The Queen Mother

Anthony Holden

A Birthday Tribute

Sphere Books Limited
London and Sydney

First published in Great Britain by Sphere Books Limited,
30–32 Gray's Inn Road, London WC1X 8JL
Copyright © Anthony Holden Ltd 1985

TRADE
MARK

This book is sold subject to the condition
that it shall not, by way of trade or otherwise,
be lent, re-sold, hired out or otherwise circulated
without the publisher's prior consent in any form of
binding or cover other than that in which it is
published and without a similar condition
including this condition being imposed
on the subsequent purchaser

Set in 11/12 pt Baskerville

Printed and bound in Great Britain by
Collins, Glasgow

ACKNOWLEDGEMENTS

Since writing a biography of the Prince of Wales five years ago, I have inevitably been asked to write about other members of the royal family for a variety of newspapers and magazines. This book grew out of one such commission from the *Sunday Express*. In the process I have made a number of friends, acquaintances and what journalists inelegantly call contacts, many of whom have helped me with my research for the present volume. As is usually the case with those around the Royal Family, they would not thank me – nor perhaps speak to me again – if I were to name them here. For my part, however, I thank them.

I must also express my gratitude for the assistance provided by members of Queen Elizabeth the Queen Mother's Household, especially Her Majesty's private secretary, Sir Martin Gilliat, and her press secretary, Major John Griffin. They are as generous in their hospitality as with their time: any visit to Clarence House invariably finishes with one, two, even three generous gin-and-tonics in the Equerry's office, a rendezvous for the Queen Mother's staff where even writers are made most welcome.

I would also like to thank Rob Shreeve, Hilary Rubinstein and Ron Hall for their advice and encouragement; Joanne Harris of Sphere Books for her picture research; Alan Samson for editing the manuscript with style and vigilance; and Deborah Holmes for her diligence as my research assistant.

From the ever-growing pile of books about the Queen Mother, I would recommend for further detail on various aspects of her life the authorised biography by Dorothy Laird (Hodder & Stoughton, 1966), and the subsequent works by Peter Lane (Hale, 1979), Elizabeth Longford (Weidenfeld, 1981), David Duff (Collins, 1983) and Ann Morrow (Granada, 1984). The fullest photographic portrait is to be found in *The Country Life Book of the Queen Mother*, with an authoritative text by Godfrey Talbot (1978, revised 1983). I have also drawn on the official biographies of King George V by Harold Nicolson (Constable, 1952) and King George VI by Sir John Wheeler-Bennett (Macmillan, 1958), and on Frances Donaldson's study of Edward VIII (Weidenfeld, 1974). Of the several volumes of memoirs quoted in the text, the most useful has been Mabel, Countess of Airlie's *Thatched with Gold* (Hutchinson, 1962).

Both my parents died, within a week of each other, while I was finishing my work on this text; suddenly, there were many echoes of their own private happiness in what I found myself writing about the strong and loving marriage chronicled in these pages. This book is therefore dedicated, with much love and many happy memories, to my mother and father.

LIST OF ILLUSTRATIONS

Photographs reproduced by gracious permission of *Her Majesty The Queen* – pages 20 bottom; 33; 38; 57 top; 78; 101; 114; 115

Times Newspapers Ltd – pages 18 inset; 75

National Portrait Gallery – page xi

BBC Hulton Picture Library – pages 8; 11; 18; 27; 49; 57 bottom; 76 top; 76 left; 76 right; 87 bottom; 89; 119; 139

Popperfoto – pages 10 top; 10 bottom; 20 top; 42 top; 42 bottom; 44; 45 top; 45 bottom; 52 top; 55; 56; 64; 65 bottom; 87 top; 93; 94 top; 95; 102; 105; 106; 108 top; 108 bottom; 121; 122; 125 top; 141 bottom; 147

Central Press – pages 34; 51 bottom; 52 top; 53; 59; 65 top; 124; 133; 138 top; 141 top; 142 bottom; 143 top; 143 bottom

Camera Press – pages 7; 12; 43; 51 top; 92 bottom; 123 top; 148

John Frost Historic Newspaper Service – page 73

Keystone – pages 92 top; 94 bottom; 123 bottom; 125 bottom; 142 top

Fox Photos – pages 99; 129; 138 bottom

Press Association – page 13

Rex Features – pages 135; 136

CONTENTS

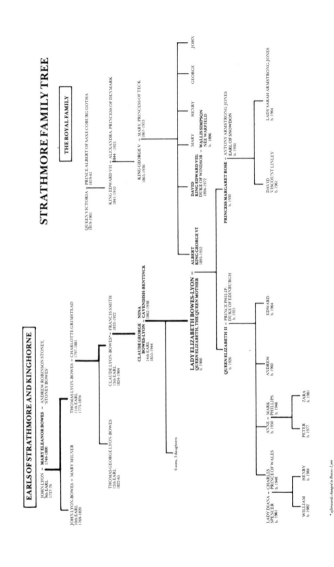

STRATHMORE FAMILY TREE

EARLS OF STRATHMORE AND KINGHORNE

THE ROYAL FAMILY

JOHN LYON = **MARY ELEANOR BOWES**
9th EARL   1749-1800
1737-76

JOHN LYON-BOWES = MARY MILNER
10th EARL
1769-1820

THOMAS LYON-BOWES = CHARLOTTE GRIMSTEAD
11th EARL
1773-1854

THOMAS GEORGE LYON-BOWES
12th EARL
1822-65

CLAUDE LYON-BOWES* = FRANCIS SMITH
13th EARL
1824-1904

ANDREW ROBINSON STONEY,
STONEY BOWES

CLAUDE GEORGE = NINA
BOWES-LYON = CAVENDISH-BENTINCK
14th EARL   1862-1938
1855-1944

QUEEN VICTORIA = PRINCE ALBERT OF SAXE COBURG GOTHA
1819-1901   1819-61

KING EDWARD VII = ALEXANDRA, PRINCESS OF DENMARK
1841-1910   1844-1925

KING GEORGE V = MARY, PRINCESS OF TECK
1865-1936   1867-1953

LADY ELIZABETH BOWES-LYON =
QUEEN ELIZABETH, THE QUEEN MOTHER
b.1900

ALBERT
KING-GEORGE VI
1895-1952

DAVID
KING EDWARD VIII
DUKE OF WINDSOR
1894-1972

MARY   HENRY   GEORGE   JOHN

WALLIS SIMPSON
NEE WARFIELD
b.1896

6 sons, 3 daughters

QUEEN ELIZABETH II = PRINCE PHILIP,
DUKE OF EDINBURGH
b.1926   b.1921

PRINCESS MARGARET ROSE = ANTONY ARMSTRONG-JONES
b.1930   EARL OF SNOWDON
                              b.1930

LADY DIANA = CHARLES
SPENCER   PRINCE OF WALES
b.1961   b.1948

ANNE = MARK
b.1950   PHILLIPS
         b.1948

ANDREW
b.1960

EDWARD
b.1964

DAVID
VISCOUNT LINLEY
b.1961

LADY SARAH ARMSTRONG-JONES
b.1964

WILLIAM   HENRY
b.1982   b.1984

PETER   ZARA
b.1977   b.1981

* Afterwards changed to Bowes-Lyon

The Reluctant Royal

The Queen Mother aged seven. This photograph was taken at Glamis Castle, her ancestral home in Scotland.

PROLOGUE

Christmas 1905, Montague House, London: at a children's party given by the Countess of Leicester, a pretty and precocious five-year-old takes pity on a painfully shy boy of ten. His name is Bertie and he happens to be the King's grandson, but he is nevertheless conspicuously ill-at-ease. To try to cheer him up, she feeds him the crystallised cherries off her sugar cake.

May 1920, 6 Grosvenor Square, London: at a society ball given by Lord and Lady Farquhar, the two meet again. The young man is now Duke of York and second in line to the throne of his father, King George V. The girl, twenty-year-old Lady Elizabeth Bowes-Lyon, ninth child of the 14th Earl of Strathmore, is the toast of society London, already being eyed by a lengthening queue of aristocratic beaux.

Not for long. Bertie cuts in on his equerry, James Stuart, MC, son of the Earl of Moray, and dances with Lady Elizabeth for the rest of the evening. That autumn, a few months later, he manages to get himself invited over from Balmoral to Glamis Castle, scene of Macbeth's murder of King Duncan, and the thousand-year-old seat of the Strathmores. He is quickly envious of their relaxed and happy home life, a stark contrast to the stern formality of his own. The evenings are spent around the piano, singing the latest Twenties songs, or playing canasta, or even charades. King George V would not have been amused.

But his second son swiftly falls in love with the Earl's youngest daughter, a half-Scottish, half-English rose of remarkable grace, wit and poise. 'The more I see of her', he writes to his mother, Queen Mary, 'the more I like her.'

A few months later, in the spring of 1921, he is ready to propose. 'You'll be a lucky fellow,' says his father, the King, 'if she accepts you.'

To everyone's dismay, she does not.

Unlike Earl Spencer's daughter sixty years later, the Earl of Strathmore's was 'frankly, doubtful' about becoming the daughter-in-law of the monarch. Like Diana Spencer she had grown up close enough to the Royal Family to see what life within it was like, but Elizabeth Bowes-Lyon reached rather different conclusions. Later that year she turned down the King's son again.

Unlike Diana, Elizabeth had little prospect of becoming Queen. Even so she was daunted by the thought of so public a life. As Bertie's aunt, Princess Alice, put it: 'None but those trained from youth for such an ordeal can sustain it with amiability and composure.'

Prince Albert did not give up. Throughout 1922 he was a frequent guest at Glamis where, in the words of one observer, 'he blossomed'. Now it was the Prince who drew confidence from this carefree family circle, and Elizabeth who grew confused. 'She was torn', said her mother, 'between her longing to make Bertie happy and her reluctance to take on the responsibilities which this marriage must bring.'

13 January 1923: In Elizabeth's favourite woods near her family's country house in Hertfordshire, the Duke of York again tries to persuade her to change her mind. This time he is spared further parental embarrassment. The King and Queen receive a wire carrying a simple, pre-arranged message: ALL RIGHT – BERTIE.

'I know I am very lucky', he wrote next day to his mother, 'to have won her over at last.'

EIGHTY-FIVE YEARS

4 August 1985: As Queen Elizabeth the Queen Mother celebrates her eighty-fifth birthday, as old as the century and still going strong, she has been a widow four years longer than she was a wife. In the autumn of her life her late husband's name is still on her lips every day, and she smilingly tells friends: 'How on earth could I ever have turned him down?'

In recent years 4 August has become an unofficial Feast Day in the crowded royal calendar – the day when the Queen Mother blushingly opens the front gate of her official London residence, Clarence House, and accepts bunches of birthday flowers from a legion of waiting admirers. She especially likes those wrapped in silver foil, or even newspaper, which she takes as a sign that they have been cut from someone's garden. The Queen and Princess Margaret are always on hand to watch, smiling but hanging back, to show that this is very much their mother's day.

For all her busy life, at an age when many in less demanding jobs have long since retired, there are three other dates in the Queen Mother's diary which her staff know to keep free each year. These are the days she withdraws from her public round, to spend a poignant few hours in the privacy of her memories. 26 April is the anniversary of her marriage to Prince Albert, Duke of York, in 1923; 14 December was his birthday and 6 February the date of his sadly premature death in 1952. They are all anniversaries of which she shuns any public commemoration.

Everywhere, in all her several homes, the memory of King George VI, her beloved 'Bertie', is kept proudly alive. The drawing room at Clarence House is bedecked with photographs and other mementoes of him. 'Not a day goes by', says

1

her private secretary of thirty years, Sir Martin Gilliat, 'without the King's name being mentioned. A great deal of thought is given to what the King would have said about this, what he would have thought about that.'

Always, on the Queen Mother's orders, 'the King'. Never, but never, 'the late King'.

The Queen Mother's life divides into three distinct phases, all of which teach us something about the art of being royal. The first – from her childhood to her marriage – shows a girl brought up in the genteel, well-heeled Scottish aristocracy, close enough to the royal family to know that its life was not for her, but nonetheless putting what she saw as her duty before her private wishes.

The second, after she had so reluctantly shouldered royal rank, shows a woman who never even wanted to be a King's in-law altered by sudden and unprecedented circumstance into a Queen: a Queen, as it transpired, for all seasons, but above all a Queen to help inspire Britons through one of the worst ordeals in their history. She may have hesitated before marrying him, but Elizabeth grew to depend on her good-hearted, strong-willed husband, whose hidden strengths of character were so drawn out by the ordeals of abdication and war. She believes, as do all who knew him, that those turbulent ten years from the crisis of 1936 to V-J Day imposed on King George VI a strain so severe that it robbed them of many more happy years together.

The third phase, which we trust is far from over, is an object-lesson in royal improvisation. There is no precedent for a Queen Dowager so visible, so active, so lively and so beloved. Even reluctant royalists, those few who cared to question the role of Britain's constitutional monarchy in the closing years of the twentieth century, even they find the Queen Mum hard to knock. For what many forget is that she is not *obliged* to do all she does. She could quite easily and justifiably have 'retired', withdrawn from public life completely, after her husband's death more than three decades ago. It was indeed the expected thing to do, as Queen Alexandra and Queen Mary, the widows of King Edward VII and King George V, had recently shown. Elizabeth was a young widow, only fifty-one, and a deeply unhappy one for many years. But she chose not merely to carve out a new royal niche for herself, which will surely prove a daunting precedent for subsequent generations. She chose to do so with an enthusiasm and an energy which are the envy of people many years younger.

'I've known her thirty years', says Sir Martin Gilliat, 'but it's still an exciting moment when I see her each morning. To the Queen Mother, every day is a new adventure.' The older she grows in years, those around her agree, the younger in spirit. At eighty-five, Queen Elizabeth is 'still wearing everyone out'.

Most octogenarians permit themselves to slow up a bit, but the Queen Mother's diary is as crowded as ever. On one typical day I visited Clarence House she had come rushing home from a luncheon engagement to chair the annual general meeting of Queen Mary's Needlework Guild, which lasted all afternoon. As she saw out her friends and colleagues, for a while just one of a crowd of elderly ladies gossiping happily in the spacious front hall, she suddenly had to excuse herself: she was due for dinner at Buckingham Palace with a visiting Head of State. Every day that week held three or four similar engagements, many involving late nights. Her Household – whom she likes to call 'my little family' – say life with the Queen Mother is 'delightful but exhausting'. It is very hard keeping up with her sheer *joie de vivre*.

She never rests in the afternoon, and after years of royal practice actually prefers standing up to sitting down. The Queen Mother can still stand for hours at a time – to the dismay of courtiers much younger, who of course have to do the same. She has never driven a car, nor been seen wearing trousers, nor smoked a cigarette, though she likes a good wine with a meal and is far from averse to a stiff gin-and-tonic – yes, ice and lemon, please – beforehand. And few things please her more than a presentation box of Bendicks' bittermints.

When spending a rare evening alone at home, she will watch television or write letters for a few hours before retiring at about eleven. A well-known fan of *Dad's Army*, she regrets the demise of light comedy shows such as *Steptoe and Son* and *All Gas and*

Gaiters. Yes, Minister has proved the only acceptable substitute in recent years – apart, of course, from the collected works of Penelope Keith. 'Her Majesty', in the words of one of her Household, 'finds little to enthuse about on television these days' – which means she has recently, in her eighties, taken to going out more in the evenings. No, she 'most certainly does *not*' watch breakfast television.

She is a great believer in a good night's sleep, rising at about nine, breakfasting in her room with *The Times, Telegraph, Mail* and *Express*, and easing into the day's work at eleven, when Sir Martin knocks on her door for their morning conference. By this time she will already have had her telephone call with her daughter, the Queen, which always begins with the greeting legendary among switchboard operators: 'Your Majesty? I have Her Majesty on the line, Your Majesty.'

There is a good hour's worth of admin., including some forty to fifty invitations, to discuss every day. The Queen Mother is patron or president of over 300 organisations, all recorded in a constantly changing little book kept in her private secretary's desk, and ranging from major institutions like the National Trust to smaller, personal favourites like the Dachshund Club. She is Colonel-in-Chief of eight regiments or service units in Britain and ten more around the Commonwealth, commandant-in-chief of all three women's services and the first female Lord Warden of the Cinque Ports.

Every year she undertakes about a hundred public engagements, arranged about six months in advance, and makes two or three overseas visits, planned a year or two ahead. There is an especially strong link with Canada, which still welcomes her every other year (right up to 1985, in the month before her eighty-fifth birthday). She regrets that political developments and the rigours of the climate have deprived her of trips to Central and Southern Africa, which she used to love, but has late in life taken to making annual, semi-private visits to France – where she exhausts her hosts, the Hennessys or the Rothschilds, with her enthusiasm for exploring châteaux.

If spending the day at home, she will often entertain either family or friends to lunch. Otherwise, she will usually share a light snack with senior members of her Household, who will have gathered beforehand in the Equerry's office for a drink or two with some wide-eyed visitors. The visitors will linger, in the distant hope of being invited to stay for lunch. But those who finally 'go through' to what is known as 'the presence' will usually include Sir Martin himself; Her Majesty's Comptroller, Sir Alastair Aird; her treasurer, Sir Ralph Anstruther; and her press officer, Major John Griffin, who typically entered her service twenty years ago as a supposedly temporary equerry. They are a devoted group, the spring chicken of whom has been with 'HM' a mere decade or three, and a vast amount of collective experience lurks beneath their officers'-mess small talk.

Sir Martin, for instance, was a Colditz escapee, but you are much less likely to hear about his war exploits than his most recent visit to the West End theatre. A 72-year-old bachelor who lives in a Hertfordshire cottage called Appletrees, Sir Martin is the focal point of the jolly, red-cheeked group of ex-military men who protect the Queen Mother in the most civilised way from the rampant demands of the outside world. The latest press indiscretion is a matter for merely momentary pre-lunch banter as Sir Martin holds court; on April Fool's Day 1985 the *Star*'s invention of a new member of the royal family was quickly disposed of as he launched into enthusiastic praise of Rowan Atkinson's performance as *The Nerd*.

If a corgi or two should intrude on these reveries, there is a sudden stiffening among all present, an instinctive straightening of ties and a rush of hands through what is left of hair – for they herald the arrival of 'the boss'.

Clarence House is the most pleasantly relaxed of all the royal residences. It is no surprise if the Queen Mother pops her head round the door as you're ensconced with one of her staff in their tiny, cramped offices, which have even more faded charm than those of Buckingham Palace. Through the walls, all the time, you can hear busy voices making eternal arrangements: perhaps HM's long-serving steward, William Tallon; or her chauffeur, John Collins; or one of the four ladies-in-waiting, whose attendance is strictly ordained by rota: Ruth, Lady Fermoy; Lady Elizabeth Basset; Lady Angela Oswald (who recently replaced Lady Jean Rankin) or Mrs Frances Campbell-Preston.

These are the elite of a forty-strong staff, the humblest of whom wear black and are cautioned to move around the house in silence. Most are devoted enough to their mistress to stay in her service for the better part of their lifetimes, despite long hours and church-mouse pay. The Queen Mother's entire public and private expenses, including the salaries of her staff, are financed from her allowance under the Civil List, raised by 3.25 per cent in Chancellor Nigel Lawson's 1985 Budget to £345,300 per annum.

As indeed are her clothes. The Queen Mother's afternoons, if no public engagements are in the diary, will perhaps include a fitting with her dressmakers (Evelyn Elliot has succeeded the legendary Sir Norman at the House of Hartnell), or with her milliners (Rudolf of Mayfair, represented by Joy Quested-Nowell). Clothes, to the Queen Mother, are 'the props' of her job; she is well aware of her reputation for light, fluffy concoctions in happy colours, with a generous sprinkling of tulle or lace. She is rarely seen without either tiara or hat – off-the-face, flowered, feathered or veiled – and never without that distinctive three-string set of pearls, which she is said to wear even while out fishing in the Dee, above a rather scruffier hat and waders.

Any free daylight hours at home are otherwise open season for portrait painters, all of whom seem remarkably un-bohemian after the drunken Augustus John. Despite having to feed him brandy as he worked, Queen Elizabeth grew rather fond of curmudgeonly old John, and still defends his portrait – which, though never finished to his satisfaction, hangs in Clarence House – against the complaints of visitors. With so many of her regiments and societies wanting official portraits and having the right to commission the artist of their choice, the Queen Mother is obliged to spend many an hour making polite conversation to total strangers. It is little wonder that royalty and portrait painters so often become firm friends

The Queen Mother was photographed on her seventy-fifth birthday by Norman Parkinson.

(Bryan Organ, for instance, recently became godfather to Prince Harry). The Queen Mother has a reputation in the artistic fraternity, as she does with press photographers, for being more co-operative than many other modern royals, and sharing a sixth sense for a good pose, with the right 'props' in place.

As I sit chatting to senior members of her staff, the phone rings with a request from Canada that the Queen Mother keep free the third week of a summer month two years hence. They'd like her to open something to do with Aberdeen Angus cattle, and visit the Toronto Irish. It sounds right up her street, so into the diary it goes. How much longer can she keep up these long-haul forays? No one dare say, beyond jocular hints that they are more worried about the toll they take on Sir Martin than the demands made on HM – who is a mere thirteen years older.

The Queen Mother's year has now developed a pretty much predestined pattern. March, for instance, means Badminton; April, a week or so of peace at Windsor. May means France; June (an especially busy month), Royal Ascot, Trooping the Colour and the annual Garter ceremony at Windsor. In late July, just before her birthday, she will base herself at

The Badminton Horse Trials, 1956. The Queen is using a cine-camera as she watches, with the Queen Mother and Princess Margaret, her horse Countryman III take a jump.

Sandringham and visit the King's Lynn Festival. And August, in her widowhood, has become synonymous in the Queen Mother's mind with the Castle of Mey, her cherished home in the far north of Scotland, on the Pentland Firth in Caithness.

The presence in her sitting room of a well-thumbed copy of *The John O'Groat's Weekly* (known to her as *The Groat*) shows how much this, her real home, remains in her thoughts all year round. Purchased after the death of her husband, as a conscious gesture towards her *vita nuova*, the sixteenth-century castle is the only home Queen Elizabeth can actually call her own. She takes great pride in her herd of Aberdeen Angus and her flock of border Cheviot sheep, driving a hard bargain at the local sales.

Most important of all: each summer, until mid-September, the Castle of Mey is the scene of house parties described by those who attend them as nothing less than 'riotous'. There is room for twelve guests, who will mostly be young people – present and past equerries and other young staff, Bowes-Lyon relations, her grandchildren and their chums, with whom she will enjoy a daily round of mackerel fishing, crab catching, remote picnics and relaxed, strictly non-dressy dinners, followed by an eightsome reel or two, even perhaps a conga.

'Life at the Castle', says an elderly visitor, 'is quite rough and ready, a bit much for people my age.' Except of course, he hastily adds, for Her Majesty. Her constantly changing round of equerries, who rarely lose touch when they return to the Army after their two-year tour of duty, means an eternal flow of devoted and dapper men in their twenties arriving with fiancées or blushing brides. The light lingers late that far north, so each evening after dinner the conga will head outside in the hope of seeing the Northern Lights – failing which, there is always the stunning view across to Orkney. Then it's back to the Dashing White Sergeants.

A cherished moment every year is the arrival on the horizon of her daughter, the Queen, on the Western Isles tour in the royal yacht, HMS *Britannia*. Many other family members will also come ashore and the day is spent, in the words of one regular participant, 'mostly ragging about'. As dusk falls and

Above: *The Queen Mother aboard the Polaris missile submarine* HMS Resolution *at the Clyde Submarine Base, 13 May 1968.* Right: *Her abiding love of Scotland frequently draws her to the Castle of Mey, her home in Caithness.* Left: *As Chancellor of the University of Dundee, the Queen Mother listens to Peter Ustinov on his installation as Rector, 20 October 1968.*

Britannia departs, the flashing of lights to and from castle and royal yacht is a touching sign to spectators that mother and daughter are bidding each other a fond farewell.

Soon to be reunited at Balmoral. While the Queen is in residence at the Castle for some ten weeks each summer, the Queen Mother will spend some time just eight miles away at Birkhall – but that once cherished home will never, like the Castle of Mey, actually belong to her. And it is still, to this day, uncomfortably full of memories of her husband. She finds herself able to enjoy them more at Royal Lodge, Windsor, where she spends every weekend she can while in London, and where the garden Bertie created is an unofficial, private monument to his memory. Now and then she will take a few days off at her much-loved childhood home, St Paul's Walden Bury, in Hertfordshire, with the widow of her youngest (and favourite) brother David.

Other close friends today – and 'close' means those likely to be invited to Windsor as weekend house-guests – include a surprising number of politicians, from the Earl of Stockton via Milords Carrington, Hailsham and Home to Sir Woodrow Wyatt, Mr Norman St John Stevas and (a particular favourite, despite HM's sternly right-wing politics) the former Labour

Members of the Royal Family take part in the Grand March at the annual Ghillies' Ball at Balmoral, 31 October 1972.

prime minister, James Callaghan. There is a strong contingent from the artistic community, notably Sir Hugh Casson, Sir Frederick Ashton, Lord David Cecil and various portrait painters; and a goodly number of fellow aristocrats, primarily the Duke and Duchess of Grafton, Lord Drogheda, Lord Charteris, the Buccleuchs, the Abercorns and the redoubtable Lady Diana Cooper.

Of her lifelong friends no longer able, alas, to enliven her house-parties, the Queen Mother particularly misses the company of Lord Clark, Lord Harlech and Sir John Betjeman. There is a phrase at Clarence House for what has happened to so many of Queen Elizabeth's relatives and friends. They have been 'gathered'; or in less reverent moments, they have 'gone upstairs'. Now in her own last years the Queen Mother loves to surround herself with young people. They keep her young, of course, but she also plays an important role in their lives.

To the younger members of the royal family, above all the Prince of Wales, she has been both confidante and friend –

especially since the murder of his beloved uncle (and 'honorary grandfather') Dickie, Lord Mountbatten. As well as being a universal mother-figure to the nation, she has become a link, a focal point for her own family's many and varied generations.

It was with the help of her closest friend, Ruth, Lady Fermoy – still, as she approaches her own eighties, one of the Queen Mother's ladies-in-waiting – that a few years ago Queen Elizabeth steered Prince Charles's amorous interests in the direction of Lady Fermoy's granddaughter, one Lady Diana Spencer. And so the Queen Mother's camp got the better of a friendly rivalry with Lord Mountbatten, who had nursed thinly disguised hopes that the heir to the throne might perhaps marry his own granddaughter, Amanda Knatchbull.

Again, in a modest way, she had helped make a little bit of history. To meet the Queen Mother, in whose person so much of this century merges, is to feast your eyes upon an icon, a face so familiar from stamps and coins, even tea towels and biscuit tins, that you are in danger of missing what she says. There are, for instance, the deep wrinkles around the eyes and down to the mouthline – the legacy of all those years of infectious smiling.

We three Queens and our fine feathers – the Queen Mother meets the Pearly Queens of Finsbury and Stoke Newington, December 1977.

There are the teeth: surprisingly, well, patchy in one so grand, until you learn that she prefers nature's way to that of expensive modern dentists. There are the eyes, a penetrating violet-blue, as lustrous now as when they broke many a noble heart in the twenties. And there is the delicate hand-clasp, a matter of firm pressure between thumb and forefinger, which she regards as part of her public duty. For the Queen Mother, it is quite a surprise to learn, has an almost pathological dislike of being touched.

However, if you can get over all these surface surprises, it is worth concentrating on the voice – a voice strangely unfamiliar, as she herself dislikes the sound of it, which is why she has so rarely broadcast. It has the famous twang of those Windsor vowels, which make houses into 'hyses' and turn girls into 'gels'. But the main thing is to listen – and you soon find yourself in an Aladdin's Cave of British history. Queen Elizabeth loves to talk about the past, despite its many lurking sadnesses; and the Queen Mother's past, to most Britons, is the story of the twentieth century.

LADY ELIZABETH BOWES-LYON

In the Indian summer of her life, a widow longer than she was a wife, Queen Elizabeth the Queen Mother has invented a royal persona unique unto herself: the Queen Dowager who does not hide herself away, a stern and remote figure like Alexandra and Mary, but a cheerful and very visible woman who has become, in her friend Cecil Beaton's words, 'this great mother-figure and nanny to us all'. At eighty-five she is as old as the century, and her story is quite as turbulent and various.

The future Queen entered the world on 4 August 1900 as another, Victoria, lay dying – worn out by years in widow's weeds and a very personal distress over the seemingly interminable course of the Boer War. Ladysmith had been relieved in February and Mafeking in May. It seems incredible now, as we behold the sprightly lady still very much with us, to recall that the year of the Queen Mother's birth was that of the Boxer Risings in China and the creation of the Commonwealth of Australia. It was the year the British Labour Party was founded. Also in 1900, Joseph Conrad published *Lord Jim*; the legendary W. G. Grace retired from cricket, with a lifetime total of 54,000 runs; the *Daily Express* was born; Puccini's opera *Tosca* had its first performance in Rome; and the Zeppelin had its first trial flight. Horseless carriages were still the preserve of a rich and eccentric few. Among those who died that year were Oscar Wilde, John Ruskin, Sir Arthur Sullivan and – much more upsetting to Victoria – King Umberto I of Italy, at the hands of an anarchist assassin.

The ninth child of Lord and Lady Glamis, heirs to the Earldom of Strathmore, Elizabeth Angela Marguerite Bowes-

Lyon was born in London on a sweltering Bank Holiday Saturday. With a sigh of relief her father retreated as quickly as possible from the metropolitan heatwave to the fresher country air of his Queen Anne home in Hertfordshire, between Welwyn and Hitchin – St Paul's Walden Bury, known to the family as 'The Bury'.

Perhaps from a sense of déjà vu, Lord Glamis proved somewhat negligent about the formalities of registering Elizabeth's birth. Oblivious to the law's demands that they be attended to within six weeks, it was not until 21 September that he presented himself at the Registrar's office in Hitchin. Even then his mind does not seem to have been entirely on the matter in hand. Before taking his newly enlarged family north for its traditional summer at Glamis, he recorded for posterity that the future Queen Consort had been born at St Paul's Walden Bury – a popular misconception ever since, reinforced by the proud but erroneous claims of a plaque in the local church, where she was indeed christened.

The truth of the matter is that no one, including the Queen Mother herself, knows exactly where in London she was born. Those few previous biographers who avoid the Hertfordshire trap tend to paint a speculative picture (as is the wont of royal biographers) of Lord Glamis pacing up and down the elegant carpets of the family's London home, 20 St James's Square, while his wife was in labour upstairs. But a little further research reveals that Lord Glamis did not take out the lease on 20 St James's Square until 1904, when he inherited his father's title and with it a considerable fortune, by which time Elizabeth was already four years old. 'London it was', remains the official line at Clarence House. 'But where? No one, including Her Majesty, will ever know.'

To complicate matters further, many of her daughter's loyal subjects still believe that the Queen Mother was born in Scotland. The fact is that, though born in England, she has always considered herself Scottish, and Scotland has duly claimed her for its own. She counts among her many and varied ancestors (one of whom was burnt as a witch) Owain Glendwyr, Prince of Wales; George Washington, first

President of the United States; but above all Robert the Bruce, King of Scotland. The family have been Lairds of Glamis Castle, just north of Dundee, since the fourteenth century, when a Lyon ancestor married Princess Joan, daughter of King Robert II, thus earning himself the title to be made notorious 300 years later by Shakespeare: Thane of Glamis.

It was not until Tudor times that the Earldom of Strathmore and Kinghorne was bestowed on the Lyon family, and not until the mid-eighteenth century that the Bowes family arrived in their midst, bringing with them at last the affluence needed to maintain those ever-growing estates. George Bowes, whose daughter Eleanor married the 19th Lord Glamis (and 9th Earl of Strathmore), was a wealthy County Durham industrialist with an eye to posterity; he transferred all his extensive property and estates in Hertfordshire and the North East to the Lyon family on the somewhat impertinent condition that it changed its surname to Bowes. This, with an eye to their finances, the Lyons duly did – but equally cannily changed it back again as soon as old Bowes died. A twinge of guilt set in with the next generation, who compromised by calling themselves Lyon-Bowes. It was not until the mid-ninteenth century that the Queen Mother's paternal grandfather, the 13th Earl of Strathmore, deemed Bowes-Lyon more felicitous.

Although she is the longest-serving Royal of our time, Lady Elizabeth Bowes-Lyon had no formal training for the rigours of royal life. As was the fashion in grand families at the dawn of the twentieth century, she had very little training for anything much at all, except the skills and graces of the well-born gentleman's wife she was expected one day to become.

When Elizabeth was just four her father inherited the Earldom of Strathmore, and with it, apart from Glamis Castle, a fortune of some £250,000 (the equivalent today, in 1985 of £8.5 million). Claud George Bowes-Lyon was a somewhat remote, old-school patrician, but a gentle and soft-hearted figure, as proud of his large walrus moustache (which he used to part like stage curtains before kissing children) as he was in later life of his elevation to the Lord-Lieutenantship of the County of Angus. Unhappy youthful experiences in the Life

Lady Elizabeth Bowes-Lyon as a three year old in the garden of St Paul's Walden Bury, her parents' Hertfordshire mansion.

Guards at Windsor Castle, where he strongly disapproved of the abandoned barrack-room behaviour of the then Prince of Wales (the future Edward VII), led the young Lord Glamis to abandon all thoughts of spending his life in the Army, like his father before him. It also led him to inculcate in his children a stout resistance, on moral rather than patriotic grounds, to any involvement with life at court.

Much more the dominant influence in her daughter's upbringing – and in the shaping of the character of the royal lady we feel we know so well today – was her mother, the former Miss Celia Cavendish-Bentinck, kinswoman to the Duke of

Portland, who had given her away at her wedding to Lord Glamis in 1881. A character sketch of the Countess of Strathmore reads uncannily like one of her daughter. A strong yet kindly character, Lady Strathmore's relaxed and informal exterior belied a disciplined and conscientious spirit, with an unquenchable zest for life. 'If there be a genius for family life,' Lady Asquith said of her, 'she has it.' A talented amateur musician, and a passionate gardener, she brought up her children to make the most of every day, herself setting them a formidable example. 'Life', she would say, 'is for living and working at. If you find anything or anybody boring, the fault lies not in them but in you.'

When she gave birth to a tenth and last child – a son, David – two years after Elizabeth, their mother called them her 'two Benjamins'. If truth be told, they were both what are known in polite society as 'surprises' – especially to parents who had already had eight children. Violet Hyacinth had been born in 1882, followed the next year by another girl, Mary Frances; then came four sons in rapid succession: John, Patrick, Alexander and Fergus. Three years later Rose Constance arrived, and three years after her, in 1893, Michael. Just seventeen days after Michael's birth their firstborn, Violet, died of diphtheria at the age of eleven.

Eight children, and one already dead. It seemed enough. But seven years later Lady Strathmore found herself with unexpected cause to be pleased that her husband had added a new wing to St Paul's to accommodate his seemingly infinite family. Then, with a certain inevitability, along came David. With all these older siblings, from seven to seventeen years older than Elizabeth, the Strathmores' two 'babies' were inseparable childhood companions, whether romping through the luxuriant woods around the Bury or exploring the castellated ramparts of Glamis.

These two main homes, though very different in atmosphere, offered equally golden childhood years for the lively-minded young Elizabeth. The Bury was a magical, rustic playground, where a menagerie of dogs and tortoises, kittens and ponies shared her adventures amid the magnolia and honeysuckle of

Lady Elizabeth Bowes-Lyon with her family at St Paul's Walden Bury. Back row, left to right: *Fergus, Jock, the 14th Earl of Strathmore, May, Pat, Alec.* Front Row: *Rose, the Countess of Strathmore holding David, Elizabeth and Michael.*

Lady Elizabeth in costume, aged nine.

the Hertfordshire countryside. Glamis Castle, though far grander and bleaker, was the setting for three summer months of family fun each year. The luxury of long sunny idylls in the heather, with her father at his most relaxed entertaining large parties of house-guests, gave Elizabeth a taste for Scottish summers which remains with her to this day. Here was born her lifelong love of fishing, which she first took up as a palatable alternative to shooting.

So when the time came for her and David's education to begin, life at Glamis was thought of as perpetual holiday while the Bury was the setting for school 'terms'. A succession of governesses came and went, but firmly in charge of the children throughout was a paragon of the proud traditions of British nannydom, Clara Cooper Knight (known to her charges as 'Alah'), daughter of a tenant farmer on the Walden Bury estate. She quickly developed a special bond with her charge, 'an exceptionally happy, easy baby, crawling early, running at thirteen months and speaking very young'. She would stay with the Bowes-Lyon family until her death at Sandringham in 1946; for when the Duchess of York, twenty years later, gave birth to her first daughter, it was 'Alah' whom she again put in charge of the nursery.

Elizabeth was a strikingly pretty and much loved – though not spoilt – little girl. Her sister Rose put it thus: 'As she was the youngest daughter, she was very much with our mother. She was such an attractive little thing that an old friend of my mother asked: "What can you do to punish Elizabeth?" My mother said, "It is enough just to say '*Elizabeth!*' in a very sad way; then she will hang her head and be sorry."'

Lady Strathmore was accounted eccentric among her friends for sending young Elizabeth to a girls' day school in London, Miss Wolff's academy in South Audley Street, for just two terms – time enough to win the school essay prize – before withdrawing her to the more normal routine of home tuition. Their mother had herself already taught them to read; now English, French and history joined music, dancing and drawing as the main subjects on each day's curriculum – when, that is, the 'two Benjamins' could be found. By the late David

Bowes-Lyon's own confession, they had a secret hideout in 'an old and half-ruined brew-house' on the Bury estate, where they fled 'whenever it seemed an agreeable plan to escape morning lessons'. In it was hidden 'a store of forbidden delicacies acquired by devious devices . . . apples, oranges, sugar, sweets, slabs of chocolate, matches and packets of Woodbines'.

Despite all this, and thanks to a French governess called Mademoiselle Lang, Elizabeth was said to be 'all but fluent' in French by the age of ten. The family motto – 'In thou, my God, I place my trust without change to the end' – was no idle slogan, for religious observance played a central part in its daily routine, whether at work, mealtimes or play. She was twelve when her much-loved brother David went away to boarding-school: 'I miss him', she confessed, 'horribly.' But at thirteen, after those two terms of her own at school, Elizabeth passed into the care of a German governess, Kathie Kuebler, who imposed a strict regime adding German and mathematics to the existing home curriculum. She was soon able to sit and pass her Junior Oxford Examination (a younger version of today's 'O' levels). At thirteen, according to her governess, she had grown 'far more mature and understanding than her years warranted'. She was 'a small, delicate figure' with 'a sensitive, somewhat pale little face, dark hair and very beautiful violet blue eyes'.

'Oh,' said Lady Buxton to her mother, 'how many hearts Elizabeth will break!' But at this point Europe was engulfed in turmoil: it was at midnight on Elizabeth's fourteenth birthday, 4 August 1914, that Asquith's deadline for a withdrawal from Belgium expired and Britain declared war on Germany. Elizabeth's annual birthday treat, a few days in the family's London home in St James's Square, and above all a trip to the theatre, was especially memorable that evening. From a box at the Coliseum she watched wide-eyed as the audience vented its patriotic fervour in a wave of excited cheers at the end of a variety show. This was the day the Foreign Secretary, Sir Edward Grey, famously declared that 'the lamps are going out all over Europe; we shall not see them lit again in our lifetime.' And life, for sure, would never be quite the same again for the teenage Elizabeth Bowes-Lyon or for any of her future subjects.

Those who still have memories of the years of calm before the First World War, including the former Lady Elizabeth Bowes-Lyon, conjure up a golden and leisurely age of perpetual summer, of gracious and tranquil living, never really to be matched thereafter. The social revolutions that inevitably follow the upheavals of war would in time consign that era to the history books. Its end was also the end of an age of innocence for this fourteen-year-old violet-eyed Scottish lass.

The effects of war on Glamis were swift and brutal. Four of Elizabeth's elder brothers immediately went to join their regiments – Patrick, John and Fergus the Black Watch, and Michael the Royal Scots. The castle itself was swiftly converted into a convalescent hospital for the war-wounded, to be run by her elder sister, Lady Rose, who took a swift nursing course in London.

Although too young to be officially on the staff, and anyway still engaged on her education by day, Elizabeth spent all her spare time cheering up the patients, who soon began to arrive from France via Dundee, and over the Sidlaw Hills to Glamis, in huge numbers. 'A Scottish Florence Nightingale,' one dubbed her, 'a tomboy who rode her bike with a cry of "Look, no hands!"' The more down-to-earth verdict on this bright-eyed young girl, whose smile had become her most infectious and striking attribute, was that she was 'a right corker'. One patient, while calling her youthful ministrations 'great medicine!', pre-echoed one of the most consistent observations made in later years about the Queen Mother: 'She always made you feel you were the one person in the world she wanted to be seeing.'

Over 1,500 men passed through Glamis during the war, many leaving memories of Lady Elizabeth on the record, but one particular story of her thoughtfulness has become famous, thanks to an account by Lady Asquith. It seems that a photograph taken by Elizabeth convinced one soldier's parents that his right arm had been amputated, because he was sitting side-on with his arm unwittingly hidden in a sling. When a friend wrote to tell him how upset his parents were, he couldn't understand why. Elizabeth, however, worked out what had happened, took another photograph to prove that his arm was still intact, and sent it to the parents with a letter apologising for causing such unnecessary concern.

Throughout those years, by Elizabeth's own account, 'My chief occupation was crumpling up tissue paper until it was so soft that it no longer crackled, to put into the lining of sleeping bags.' Otherwise, the war meant simply 'knitting, knitting, knitting'.

Rows of beds lined the stately ancestral halls of Glamis, at least one of which was reputed to house an ancient, ghostly monster. In stark contrast to those familiar summer sounds of cricket, croquet and laughter from the garden, the descants of Elizabeth's life that autumn were the low moans of men who had suffered appalling wounds in the trenches. Where once the clack of billiard balls had enlivened weekend house-parties, the tables were now piled high with old clothes to be converted into makeshift 'comforters'. At Christmas especially, the enthusiastic hospitality of the Bowes-Lyon family helped a new and less fortunate brand of house-guest temporarily to forget his woes.

The family itself was not spared its share of personal wartime tragedy. Less than a year after the birth of his own daughter, Elizabeth's brother Fergus fell in the Battle of Loos, a calamity from which their mother never really recovered. The Bowes-Lyons lived in constant dread of another such telegram, which duly arrived in early 1917 when the War Office reported Michael dead in action. Young David, summoned home from Eton to join the family's mourning, refused to wear black and confidently declared he had seen his elder brother in a dream, 'in a big house surrounded by fir trees . . . not dead, but very ill, because his head is tied up in a cloth'. David's powers of clairvoyance were duly and joyfully vindicated three months later, when Michael was discovered to be a prisoner-of-war – suffering, indeed, from a shrapnel wound to the head.

And so the grim years of conflict wound on, with the ever more mature Elizabeth taking an increasingly substantial role in the running of Glamis, especially once Lady Rose left to be married in 1916. She helped her patients write letters home, took copious photographs for them to enclose, went shopping for them in the village, and cheered them with constant games of cards and tunes at the piano. As her mother's health began to fail and her schooldays came to an official end, she was in fact in unofficial and unconscious training for a lifetime of public service.

One such initiative at this time led Lady Elizabeth indirectly into the royal circles which would one day become her permanent home. Wartime had brought the Bowes-Lyons into an even closer association with the community around Glamis, where Elizabeth's special enthusiasm was the Girl Guides. After growing out of the movement, she remained one of its patrons and supporters – and thus first met and formed a lasting friendship with the King's only daughter, Princess Mary. It was inevitable that she was soon invited to the Palace to meet her new friend's parents and her eldest brother, the dashing young Prince of Wales.

Throughout her childhood, summer visitors to Glamis had nicknamed Elizabeth 'Princess' – a rank she had at times jokingly accorded herself. In 1903, after a weekend at the castle the Duchess of Atholl wrote: 'I was very impressed by the charm and dignity of a little daughter, two or three years old, who came into the room looking as if a little princess had stepped out of an eighteenth-century picture.' And six years later, in 1909, the Rev. James Stirton, vicar of Glamis, told of a garden party at which this captivating nine-year-old had danced to a piano accompaniment by her mother. When he went over to congratulate her and ask her name, she replied with that soon-to-be-famous smile: 'I call myself the Princess Elizabeth!' That the family could so sustain so risqué a joke so long shows how far from their thoughts was any notion that it might one day come true.

By the war's end Elizabeth was eighteen, naturally mature for her years but the more so by virtue of living with the terrible consequences of conflict around her during those formative years. Glamis remained a hospital even after the Armistice was signed, a staging-post for wounded Australian and New

Zealand officers awaiting their passage home. But 1920 saw smart society gradually picking up its natural rhythms again – a giddy round of country house weekends and, for the gels, ascending to 'town' to 'come out' amid the renewed social whirl. The debutante Lady Elizabeth, according to her husband's biographer, Sir John Wheeler-Bennett, 'took London by storm', though her mother's friend Lady Airlie was shrewd enough to note that she was 'very unlike the cocktail-drinking, chain-smoking girls who came to be typical of the Twenties'.

Lady Asquith noticed too: 'Her natural sense of responsibility – a cheerful and not a self-righteous one – was fostered both by her upbringing and the war. A sense of responsibility is undeniably a burden, and the fact that she never tried to shift any weight from her young shoulders explains why, at the age of eighteen, for all its gaiety, the observant saw on her face a look of experience beyond her years.'

As the *jeunesse dorée*, starved of four years of frolics and fun, threw themselves into a decade of wild abandon, Elizabeth preferred the quieter, more decorous pace of life as it had been lived before the war. Royal Ascot, country weekends and the grand ballrooms of her friends' London houses were more her natural circuit than the night-clubs and all-night parties of so many of her contemporaries. She was not, in short, a 'modern' girl. But if the Bowes-Lyons' style of life and dress remained in some ways a little behind the times, they were a robust and down-to-earth family who loved nothing so much as to enjoy themselves and to entertain. One of Elizabeth's beaux spoke of life at Glamis immediately after the war as 'like living in a Van Dyck picture. Time stood still . . .' And of the Lady Elizabeth: 'I fell madly in love with her. We all did.'

Now she began the unhappy, quite involuntary process of breaking many a noble heart. 'Her radiant vitality and a blending of gaiety, kindness and sincerity made her irresistible to me,' wrote Lady Airlie. A veritable pack of eligible young bachelors, many of them newly returned war heroes, began to pursue her around the hectic social calendar – until one May evening in 1920 it reached the Grosvenor Square home of Lord

Alexandra, Lady Airlie, in 1922. A close and valued friend of both Prince Albert and Lady Elizabeth. Her Scottish castle, Cortachy, was a significant location for their courtship.

Farquhar, Master of the King's Household in the reign of Edward VII. Here, as legend has it, it was Lady Annally, a mutual friend, who enjoyed the privilege of effecting the historic introduction.

Prince Albert was twenty-four, Lady Elizabeth nineteen. Lady Airlie, a close and increasingly valued friend to both, reported: 'He told me long afterwards that he had fallen in love that evening, although he did not realise it until later.' Elizabeth gave no sign of noticing the royal ardour and continued the season with an open mind, in no great hurry to find herself a husband. Lady Cynthia Colville, ruminating on another passing attachment, knew why: 'The unusually attractive and popular Elizabeth had so many devoted admirers that she found it difficult to decide upon which to bestow her favour; not because she was flirtatious, but because she felt that marriage was desperately important and irrevocable.'

Lady Airlie had sensed this too: 'One knew instinctively that she was a girl who would find real happiness only in marriage and motherhood. A born homemaker.' Her ladyship became something of a confidante to both. 'They started dropping in at my flat, on various pretexts, always separately but each talked of the other. She was frankly doubtful, uncertain of her feelings and afraid of the public life which would lie ahead of her as the King's daughter-in-law . . . 'The Duke's humility was touching. He was deeply in love but so humble.' The King, his father, had granted Prince Albert the title of Duke of York just two weeks after he had met Elizabeth at the Farquhars. It is clear that George V already held a high opinion of Bertie's sense of duty, the more so because of his elder brother's increasingly frequent lapses from grace. The Queen, meanwhile, seems to have noticed her son's feelings for Lady Elizabeth almost before he himself had fully interpreted them. When Lloyd George told the King that the country would not tolerate a foreign alliance for the Prince of Wales and that the Duke of York should also look for a bride among the British aristocracy, Queen Mary told Lady Airlie: 'I don't think Bertie will be sorry to hear that. I have discovered that he is very much attracted to Lady Elizabeth Bowes-Lyon. He's always talking about her.'

Was it coincidence, or was it as a moist-eyed go-between that Lady Airlie invited Princess Mary to her own Scottish castle, Cortachy, in that summer of 1920 – and suggested that her brother, the Duke of York, might like to join them? Given Elizabeth's growing friendship with Mary, and the Earl of Strathmore's penchant for crowding Glamis with well-born weekenders, it was inevitable that they would all be invited over and that Bertie would get a chance to take a closer look at the object of his affections, in the relaxed and informal atmosphere of her own natural habitat. So much more relaxed and informal than his own, in fact, that his enjoyment of it only deepened his feelings for Elizabeth. As his official biographer, Wheeler-Bennett, put it: 'The relations of Lord and Lady Strathmore with their children and the happy badinage and affection of a large and close-knit family were a revelation to him, providing a climate of ideas to which he instantly responded and in which his own personality throve and blossomed.' The Prince himself wrote to Queen Mary: 'It is delightful here, and Elizabeth is very kind to me. The more I see her, the more I like her.'

In retrospect, it is clear that many other pairs of eminent eyes were watching equally closely. When poor Bertie was turned down for the first time the following spring – having made the mistake of telling his parents in advance that he was going to propose – he was not the only one to be disappointed. Everyone respected Lady Elizabeth's demure reluctance to be royal, but to those shrewd older eyes who had watched her grow up she seemed to be sacrificing the chance of a marriage made in heaven. 'I do hope he will find a nice wife who will make him happy,' said Lady Strathmore of the 'disconsolate' Duke of York. 'I like him so much, and he is a man who will be made or marred by his wife.' Queen Mary and Lady Airlie, meanwhile, positively seethed with disappointment.

One hesitates, at a distance of more than sixty years, to take too strong a line on the determined matchmaking of these noble ladies, but one has to record that the Queen duly invited herself to Lady Airlie's Cortachy Castle that summer, a few months after Elizabeth's first rejection of Bertie – and took her son along too. No sooner had she arrived than she issued a royal command that they be invited next to Glamis.

With her mother ill – she had never really recovered her health since the loss of Fergus – Elizabeth was acting as hostess. She did so with such grace and aplomb that it has even been rumoured that the Queen enjoined George V to add Elizabeth's name to their secret list of suitable brides for the Prince of Wales. This seems most unlikely, however, for the Queen confided at the time in her friend Lady Airlie that she had become ever more convinced that this was 'the one girl who could make Bertie happy'. But she decided to say nothing to either of them. 'Mothers', declared this fond old meddler, 'should never meddle in their children's love affairs.'

Lady Airlie begged to differ. 'As the Duke was not my son', she reasoned, 'I might be permitted a little discreet meddling.

Although the romance seemed at an end, I continued to plead his cause from time to time.' Elizabeth continued to visit her and listened sympathetically to her arguments, but she remained steadfast in her attitude. Early in 1922 she had a taste of royal life as a bridesmaid at Princess Mary's wedding to Lord Lascelles, the first full-blown state ceremonial since the war, and that summer she again entertained an entreating Bertie at Glamis. His only consolation was that while she turned down his proposals she was turning down numerous others as well that year. But she had grown so fond of him, and had been made so privy to his feelings for her, that her position became ever more painful. 'That winter', said her mother, 'was the first time I have ever known Elizabeth to be really worried.'

After suffering most of her agonies at Glamis, it was at St Paul's Walden Bury, the following spring, that Elizabeth finally succumbed. It was clearly shrewd of Bertie to suggest a walk in her favourite woods, scene of so many of her happiest childhood memories, where every association was of things going right. But none of those who so copiously chronicle the course of the affair for us, not even Lady Airlie, offer any further theories as to why Elizabeth at last changed her mind. We are left with the obvious assumption that her own kindness of heart, combined with the growing strength of her attachment to this very decent, honest and devoted young man, finally took on more significance than her continuing horror of surrendering her privacy, independence and to some extent her personal identity to the unenviable fate of life in the royal goldfish-bowl, where the water was then much colder than it is today.

She is said to have confided in a friend in later years: 'It was my duty to marry Bertie, and I fell in love with him afterwards.' But any lingering doubts were characteristically swallowed that day as she wholeheartedly and unselfishly shared the Prince's infectious joy. 'My dream has at last been realised,' he wrote to Elizabeth's mother. 'It seems too marvellous to me that my darling Elizabeth will one day be my wife. We are both very, very happy, and I am sure always will be.'

A stark contrast to the previous summer when the house-guests at Glamis, apart from the Duke of York, had included the American-born Conservative MP now better remembered as a diarist, 'Chips' Channon. Rain had prevented the usual outdoor exertions one day, so Channon found himself joining a bridge four with Bertie and the object of his tortured affections. Himself rather in love with her, enamoured especially of 'her curious sideways lilting walk', Channon suddenly made a great show of reading his cards intently and telling the Lady Elizabeth's fortune. 'I predict', he announced, 'a great and glamorous royal future for Lady Elizabeth.' His hostess had laughed lightly as she led the other guests upstairs to change for dinner, but Bertie remained uncomfortably behind, unable to hide from his mortified fellow guests the agonies of his only partially requited love.

Six months later, when Elizabeth finally accepted her Prince's third proposal, Channon confided in his diary with his usual candour: 'There is not a man in England today who doesn't envy him. The clubs are in gloom.'

DUCHESS OF YORK

Enter Prince Albert; exit, hastily, all other suitors.

On 15 January 1923, two days after he had at last been accepted, the Duke of York took tea with his parents. Bertie, the King recorded in his diary that night, 'informed us that he was engaged to Elizabeth Bowes-Lyon, to which we gladly gave our consent. I trust they will be very happy.' Queen Mary recorded in hers: 'We are delighted, and he looks beaming.'

Next day the engagement was officially announced in the Court Circular, and Bertie (who had picked up his father's habit of never using a conjunction when an ampersand would do) wrote to his mother: 'You & Papa were both so charming to me yesterday about my engagement, & I can never really thank you properly for giving your consent to it. I am very happy & can only hope that Elizabeth feels the same as I do.'

This was more than merely the customary thanks from a relieved son to parents good enough to approve his choice of bride. Bertie was the first royal prince to have chosen a 'commoner', and one of pure British stock, since the future King James II (when also Duke of York) had married Lady Anne Hyde, daughter of the Duke of Clarendon, nearly 300 years before. The engagement set a royal precedent to be much quoted and copied as the century progressed, so that nearly fifty years later the heir to the throne himself was able to marry a commoner – another Earl's daughter, the Lady Diana Spencer.

King George V looked with disfavour on the 'flappers' of the 1920s. A man's man with four sons – Edward, Prince of Wales; Albert, Duke of York; George, Duke of Kent; and Henry, Duke of Gloucester – he anyway regarded with considerable unease

Lady Elizabeth photographed at the time of her betrothal to the Duke of York in January 1923.

Lady Elizabeth visited Edinburgh with the Duke of York before their wedding and received a particularly warm reception.

the whole prospect of 'so many daughters-in-law'. So it was characteristically loyal of *The Times* of the day to share His Majesty's relief that his first was so distinctly and proudly 'unmodern'. In a leading article which had the sauce to declare, *en passant*, that 'her figure is that of a woman, not the flat boyish outline so much admired today', the 'Top People's paper' got quite carried away: 'She has wonderful skin and hair. But her greatest charm is her voice. It is like cream and honey turned into sound, and the listener is hypnotised by its musical quality . . . Although serenity is the keynote of Elizabeth's character, as with all the women of the Strathmore family she has also a Scot's shrewdness. She is intensely home-loving. Perhaps that is one of her chief charms for her husband-to-be. From her mother she inherits the house-wifely qualities of the Dutch . . .'

Etcetera etcetera. As Fleet Street's sickly-sweet accolades rolled over her, much as she had feared, Elizabeth displayed the kind of pre-royal naivete more recently associated with Prince Charles's bride when she innocently gave her first interview to a newspaper reporter. It was a Mr Harry Cozens-Hardy of *The Star* (no relation to the sheet of that name which exists today) who had penetrated the front hall of the Strathmores' new London home in Bruton Street. He was being given short shrift by the butler when Elizabeth appeared on the scene 'with the most radiant face that the purlieus of Bond Street had ever seen'.

Mr Cozens-Hardy had good reason for such tabloid lyricism, as the Princess-to-be proceeded to tell Lady Strathmore, who was attempting to intervene, 'Mother, leave this gentleman to *me*.' He went on to describe how, 'seated at a little writing desk, pen in hand, with letters and telegrams before her', the newly engaged Elizabeth 'tactfully' remarked, 'I suppose you have come to congratulate me? How very kind of you.'

He hadn't, of course. He had come to ask if it was true, as rumoured, that the Duke of York had found it necessary to propose three times before gaining her acceptance. 'Gracefully', as he put it, she cunningly replied: 'Now look at me. Do you think I am the sort of person Bertie would have to ask twice?'

As soon as the first editions of the next day's *Star* appeared, the first newspaper interview Lady Elizabeth had ever given also became, on the urgent orders of the King, the last.

This endearing indiscretion was, however, a mere hiccough in Elizabeth's swift and total triumph in winning the heart of her fiancé's fearsome father. Later that month, after she and her parents had spent a weekend at Sandringham with the King and Queen, in the equally daunting presence of Queen Alexandra, George V confided to his diary: 'She is a pretty and charming girl & Bertie is a very lucky fellow.' Queen Mary, for

35

her part, could express her relief that the longed-for match had at last materialised: 'Elizabeth is so charming, so pretty & engaging & natural', she wrote. 'Bertie is supremely happy.'

This was no idle boast. No one who knew Prince Albert had ever seen him quite so contented and self-assured. His life hitherto had been a largely awkward, painful history of hesitancy and self-doubt, thanks in part to a deep-dyed dread of his father, and in part to the ordeal of having to live in the perpetual shadow of a more brilliant, more handsome elder brother. His stammer, an acutely embarrassing affliction which haunted everything from his public speeches to his private conversation – even his proposals to Elizabeth Bowes-Lyon – was a mixture, it would seem, of cause and effect.

Even Bertie's arrival in the world had been singularly ill-timed. He was born in 1895, at 3 am on 14 December, thus intruding by a few hours into the day hallowed by Queen Victoria as the most sacred of her annual calendar of obsessive mourning – the 'terrible anniversary' of the death in 1861 of her beloved husband and consort, Prince Albert. Rather than celebrate, the new Prince's father felt obliged to apologise to his grandmother for such monstrous thoughtlessness. Warned by his father, Edward VII, that 'Grandmama was rather distressed that this happy event should have taken place on a darkly sad anniversary,' the future George V, then himself Duke of York, wrote to the Queen: 'I am afraid, dear Grandmama, you were rather distressed that he was born on the 14th, that doubly sad day to you and all our family, but we hope that his having been born on that day may be the means of making it a little less sad to you . . .'

There followed a masterstroke, sure to win the old lady's blessing on the hapless infant. 'Dear Grandmama,' George went on, 'we propose with your permission to call him *Albert* after dear Grandpapa.' He added his hope that the Queen would consent to be the child's godmother – which she did – but for the rest of his life remained unconvinced that Victoria had ever forgiven either him or his second son, occasionally confiding to friends that she had regarded the birth as 'a personal affront'. The most generous remark on record from the Queen was a note in her diary about the date of his birth: 'I have a feeling that it might be a blessing for the dear little boy, and may be looked upon as a gift from God.' Had she known that his coronation as sovereign would take place exactly 100 years after her own, Victoria would no doubt have felt that subsequent, unexpected events vindicated her belief in divine intervention.

Bertie was the second son of a kind and good father, but a father prone to notoriously bad relations with his children. 'My father was frightened of his mother, I was frightened of my father, and I am damned well going to see to it that my children are frightened of me,' George V told his friend Lord Derby. He always insisted, for instance, that Bertie, though naturally left-handed, write with his right; and when the prince was found to have knock knees, he was made to wear splints which caused him such pain that he lost sleep and could not concentrate on his schooling. 'There seems to have been an emotional quality in [George V's] feeling for his children', wrote Edward VIII's biographer, Frances Donaldson, 'which made him irritable as well as anxious, hostile as well as affectionate.'

He may have said he was frightened of him, but George V had in Edward VII a warm and loving father, whose role he conspicuously failed to recreate with his own children. All his life he treated his family as if it were a ship's company, of which he was both master and martinet. 'We were, in fact, figuratively speaking, always on parade,' wrote the Duke of Windsor in his memoirs. 'If we appeared before him with our Navy lanyards a fraction of an inch out of place, or with dirks or sporrans awry, there would be an outburst worthy of the quarterdeck of a warship.' When they were seen with their hands in their trouser pockets, their nanny was told to sew the pockets up.

His father, at first, was however the least of Prince Albert's problems. Born at his parents' weekend and holiday home, York Cottage, he spent much of his early life at this most unlikely of royal residences – a pokey rabbit-warren of a place on the Sandringham estate, furnished in so rudimentary a way that an appalled Harold Nicolson described it in his diary as

Prince Albert, the second son of King George V and Queen Mary, aged ten in 1905, the year he first met Lady Elizabeth Bowes-Lyon at a children's party given by the Countess of Leicester. The sailor rig anticipates his time in the Royal Navy.

'indistinguishable from any Surbiton or Upper Norwood home'. Here for the first few years of his life he had a nanny, subsequently found to be mentally unstable, who developed a preference for his elder brother and victimised poor Bertie, feeding him so inadequately that he developed a chronic weakness of the stomach. He was much happier under her replacement, the under-nurse, Mrs Bill, but she too was suddenly dismissed when he was seven, and his father returned from a tour of Australia to be appalled by a breakdown in discipline (largely encouraged, if truth be known, by the children's much less authoritarian grandfather, Edward VII).

All George V's children are said to have been of nervous or highly-strung dispositions, but none more so than Bertie, who was from the youngest age described as 'easily frightened and somewhat prone to tears'. It was on Mrs Bill's departure that he first developed his stammer – a most extreme form of that unfortunate affliction, which could at times reduce him to virtual speechlessness. Given also a share of his father's inclination to sudden rages, he was soon said to be 'volatile' and 'mercurial', prone to 'outbursts of emotional excitement – sometimes of high spirits and exuberance, sometimes of passionate weeping and depression' – and 'squalls of temper which, though of brief duration, left him exhausted in both body and mind'.

These fits of rage grew worse when their father hired as tutor to Bertie and his brother Mr H. P. Hansell, an exemplary Norfolk sportsman whose only shortcoming, it would seem, was that he couldn't teach. Above all he proved quite unable to communicate any grasp of mathematics, an indispensable subject for the entrance exams to the Royal Naval College, whither they were bound at their father's behest. Despair would seize hold of Bertie, says his official biographer, 'as problem after problem resisted his efforts to solve them, and he would ultimately dissolve into angry tears'.

Both princes, hardly surprisingly, were nevertheless ad-mitted to Dartmouth, where Bertie came 71st out of 71 at the end of his first-year exams, rising at best to 61st out of 67. But he was happier here than at any previous time of his life; away from the authoritarian atmosphere of his home, living for the first time with people his own age, he began to make friends with whom at times he even grew relaxed enough not to stammer.

'One could wish', wrote Prince Albert's tutor to his father, 'that he had more of Prince Edward's keenness and application.' That Bertie grew up in the constant shadow of his brother was later acknowledged by no one so much as that brother himself. 'The only thing that saved me from my father's wrath', he used to say when Duke of Windsor, 'was that, however badly I did, Bertie could be relied on to do worse.' So it was only when their ways parted – Bertie to join the wartime Navy, Edward (who could not take such risks) to be trained for kingship – that the younger brother really began to flourish.

Still he was dogged by illness. Once aboard his first battleship, HMS *Collingwood*, this seemingly jinxed young man found himself prone to seasickness. But a persistent, deeply depressing state of ill health seemed to go deeper than that; in fact it was a duodenal ulcer, which would not be diagnosed and removed for some years. When his Captain tentatively suggested to his father, via his private secretary, that the Prince be given sick-leave and treated ashore in a nursing home, he was told: 'The King would prefer to run the risk of Prince Albert's health suffering than that he should endure the lasting and bitter disappointment of not being in his ship in the battle line.'

'Mr Johnson', as he was discreetly known, was thus in a state of some despair in *Collingwood*'s sick bay when a signal was received that the German fleet was engaging English battle cruisers only forty miles away. The Battle of Jutland, in fact, was moving in *Collingwood*'s direction. The Prince's friend, Lieutenant Campbell Tait, described what happened next: 'Huge excitement. Full speed ahead. Sound of action – can you imagine the scene! Out of his bunk leaps "Johnson". Ill? Never felt better! Strong enough to go to his turret and fight a prolonged action. Of course he was, why ever not?' As Sir John Wheeler-Bennett confirms: 'To his turret he went, to remain there until the guns were firmly secured the next day.'

Jutland was the making of Prince Albert, as were the Falklands for another royal second son two generations later. There may have been, as with Prince Andrew, more false starts to follow his apparent transition from tentative youth to macho manhood; but for a while at least he managed with much greater success to realise his father's hopes of him. He went on to distinguish himself in the Navy; then in the RAF, where he took charge of training at Cranwell, and served in France and Belgium; on the tennis courts, where he won the RAF doubles at Wimbledon with his friend Louis Grieg; and at Cambridge, where he showed much more application, particularly in his studies of the constitution, than had his elder brother at Oxford. After the war he began to become a popular public figure, largely through his work for youth – notably through the Duke of York's camps – and for youth training through the Industrial Welfare Association. He became a good horseman and an excellent shot. It was thus a less diffident, if still stammering Prince who had met and wooed Lady Elizabeth Bowes-Lyon in the early 1920s.

Their wedding, on 26 April 1923 in Westminster Abbey, was the first of a King's son in the Abbey since the future Richard II had married Princess Anne of Bohemia there 540 years before. A proposal from the British Broadcasting Corporation that the service be broadcast was vetoed by the Dean and Chapter, on the grounds that 'people might hear it while sitting in public houses, with their hats on'. So no sound record of the occasion exists. But the film taken that day amply testifies to the visible and very genuine happiness of the occasion.

'A princely marriage', in the words of Walter Bagehot, the historian of the British constitution, 'is the brilliant edition of a universal fact, and as such it rivets mankind.' The Yorks made a handsome couple, and the nation was *en fête*, with renewed attention focused on the best man, the bridegroom's elder brother David. When would *he*, the Prince of Wales, be getting married and starting a family? No one, least of all the happy couple themselves, thought for a moment that day they were celebrating the marriage of a future King and Queen.

Top: *Lady Elizabeth, on her last morning as a commoner, leaves her parents' London home, 17 Bruton Street, for her marriage in Westminster Abbey to the Duke of York on 26 April 1923.* Above: *The Princess Royal, Princess Maude, Queen Alexandra, Queen Mary, the bride and bridegroom on the balcony at Buckingham Palace on their return from Westminster Abbey.*

After the wedding Buckingham Palace was the scene of a series of official photographs.

The Duke and Duchess of York in conversation at a game of polo, 1923.

Top: *The new Duchess of York leaves Buckingham Palace with her husband for the first part of their honeymoon at Polesden Lacey in Surrey.* Above: *The Duchess chances her arm at the coconut shy during a visit to Loughton in Essex, 1923.*

Though David still cut more of a dash, Bertie now for the first time found his own place in the public's hearts. That the British had come to sympathise with the illness and bad luck which had dogged his life hitherto, especially during the war, was witnessed by a touching wedding-day tribute in a special supplement of *The Times*: 'Young as he is, and great as is his station, he has known enough of frustration to make all admirers of pluck and perseverance the more anxious to wish him success and happiness.' And the Archbishop of Canterbury, Cosmo Lang, took time during the service to offer the Duke a personal tribute – echoed by the many outside who had brushed shoulders with him on his factory rounds or exchanged words with him at his camps: 'You, Sir, have already given many proofs of your care for the welfare of our working people. You have made yourself at home in the mines and shipyards and factories. You have brought the boys of the workshop and the public school together in free and frank companionship. You have done much to increase the public sense of the honour and dignity of labour.'

The King, too, in a private letter to his son, thought this aspect of his royal duties worth a touching mention: 'By your quiet, useful work you have endeared yourself to the people, as was shown on Thursday by the splendid reception they gave you.' Bertie's father, showing the kind heart which had always lurked behind the gruff, growling exterior, also told his son he would miss him 'very much' – and why. 'You have always been so sensible & easy to work with & you have always been ready to listen to any advice & to agree with my opinions about people & things, that I feel we have always got on very well together...

'Very different', the King added in pained parentheses, 'to dear David.' *The Times* seemed equally pained as it perversely chose to mark the Yorks' wedding day with the view – perhaps a coded message inspired by a worried courtier – that 'another royal wedding, that of the Prince of Wales, would be even more welcome'.

The honeymoon began, as is traditional to this day in royal circles, at the home of friends, the Mr and Mrs Ronald

Grevilles, at Polesden Lacy, near Dorking. The newly-weds then moved on to Glamis, where the bride developed whooping-cough ('so unromantic', she wrote to Queen Mary) and Frogmore, where Bertie found his happiness dimmed only by memories of his schooldays with Hansell. Otherwise they were lazy, carefree days during which the deep and abiding significance of the changes wrought by marriage began to sink into both of them. Wheeler-Bennett describes the Duke of York's marriage as nothing less than 'the first great climacteric of his life'.

Without mincing his words, the royal family's choice as George VI's biographer goes on to explain: 'Not only did it entail emancipation from a home environment which, despite the sentiments of his father's letter, had not been entirely congenial to him, but it brought him much for which he had long craved in deprivation – love, understanding, sympathy, support. All these things were now his in generous abundance, and his whole conspectus of life changed accordingly.'

Elizabeth's family, for their part, had begun to realise that their lovingly secure domestic background had in fact prepared her perfectly, if inadvertently, for the royal way of life. She was already a gracious hostess – the summer of Bertie's first proposal, after all, she had become temporary *châtelaine* of Glamis during her mother's illness – but she also knew from her wartime experiences how to care about people, offer them comfort and concern, communicate a warm and powerful sense of her own joy in living. Today, six decades later, these are the qualities with which her daughter's subjects still credit her; at the time, they were the not-so-small mercies on which her new husband would rely through the unforeseen troubles ahead.

It was also striking that Elizabeth got on better with the fearsome King George V than any of his own children. Elizabeth was never, like them, afraid of him, nor he apparently concerned to make her so. She did not share his children's dread of his stern, antiquated demands, sharing rather his feeling for traditional custom and practice. Even his obsession with punctuality was relaxed for this much-prized new daughter-in-law (who all her life has considered clocks and watches rather irritating distractions from the more important niceties of her daily timetables). Once, when she apologised for arriving late at the dinner table, the King astonished the rest of the table by saying 'Not at all, my dear. We must have sat down too early.' He later explained: 'Ah, but if she weren't late, she would be perfect, and how horrible that would be.'

The Yorks, having started married life in the cold, gaslit, no-mod-cons discomfort of White Lodge, Richmond Park (today the Royal Ballet School), were soon happily ensconced in 145 Piccadilly, with the use of Royal Lodge, Windsor, as a weekend retreat. With the pregnant Princess Mary's withdrawal from public life, and the death of Princess Christian, Queen Victoria's third daughter, the new Duchess found herself very much in demand as patron of this, president of that, and was thrown into the deep end of the royal routine rather more suddenly than the King would have wished. 'We must try', he said, 'to break her in slowly.' He needn't have worried. 'She lays a foundation stone', wrote *The Times*, 'as though she had just discovered a new and delightful way of spending an afternoon.'

Her main contribution as yet, however, would be a private one – to her husband, giving him the confidence he had so long lacked, helping him through the public engagements, especially speaking engagements, which he dreaded, sustaining him by a smile or a gesture through his appalling public battles with his stammer. It was at her insistence, in 1926, that the Duke of York first went to a Harley Street specialist named Lionel Logue, who persuaded him that his stammer was associated with his breathing, not his powers of speech, still less his mind. This advice appears to have been a turning-point in the Duke's life. After beginning a series of deep-breathing exercises prescribed by Logue, he was able to write to his father: 'I have been seeing Logue every day & have noticed a great improvement in my talking, & also in making speeches which I did this week . . . I wish I could have found him before, as now that I know the right way to breathe my fear of talking will vanish.'

It was with a new sense of self-confidence that the Duke of

The opening of the British Empire Exhibition at Wembley, 10 May 1925. The Duchess of York is with her mother, the Countess of Strathmore, and her husband's younger brother, Prince George.

York set out with his wife on their first official overseas journeys, to Yugoslavia, Northern Ireland, East Africa and the Sudan – preparation for the round-the-world expedition traditional after a royal marriage. In the autumn of 1925, however, the Duchess discovered she would first have a much more important event to concentrate on. She was carrying their first child.

Princess Elizabeth Alexandra Mary was born at the Strathmores' London home in Bruton Street, by Caesarean section, in the early hours of 21 April 1926. Too late for that day's newspapers, the news of this royal birth was the first to reach the waiting world through the newly fashionable medium of the wireless. Next day's papers anyway chose to give the King's first grandchild second billing to the latest developments in the General Strike; she was scarcely likely to have much impact on the line of succession, once her Uncle David had married and begun a family, and indeed once her own parents had bred a few male children.

When Princess Margaret Rose was born at Glamis four years later, there was renewed public delight – as against a degree of royal disappointment that the child was not a prince – but the same lack of constitutional interest. George V was pleased to have some grandchildren, even if they were female. He asserted himself only by vetoing the Duchess of York's preferred name of Ann, for reasons he never chose to reveal; Elizabeth was to be delighted when her own daughter made good the omission by inscribing the name on the Windsor family tree a quarter of a century later. In general the toddling princesses attracted little attention and were able to spend those important first few years of their lives in comparative privacy, comfortably out of reach of the spotlight which was all too soon to descend upon the Yorks.

By the time of Margaret's birth, her parents had become seasoned royal troupers. The length of their world tour in 1927 reminds us that these were still the days of the British Empire; the prospect of seven months away from her six-month-old baby upset the Duchess so much that their car had to circle Grosvenor Square several times on their departure to enable her to regain her composure for the official scenes of farewell.

In Australia and New Zealand, the Duke of York had to overcome ill-disguised advance disappointment that the King's representative was not to be the popular Prince of Wales, veteran of several barnstorming visits; he and his Duchess did so to such effect that, back home, George V was besieged with reports praising their natural, human touch. 'The Prince of Wales', reported one colonial governor, 'had been phenomenally feted and popular, yet almost everywhere people had liked the Duke of York better. This was not the opinion I had expected, so I cross-questioned them closely on this. "This fellow's trying to do his job better," came the reply.'

Elizabeth had played an indispensable role in what was an important personal triumph for Bertie, an invaluable boost to his ever shakey morale. She could often be seen chivvying and encouraging him, especially when there was a speech to make. A turning-point came in New Zealand's South Island, when she developed tonsilitis. The Duke wanted to cancel the rest

Top: *The Christening of Princess Elizabeth of York, 29 May 1926.* Left to right: *Lady Elphinstone, the Duke of Connaught, Queen Mary, King George V, the Duchess of York with Princess Elizabeth, the Duke of York, the Countess and Earl of Strathmore, and Viscountess Lascelles. None present could have predicted that there were two future Queens of England in their midst.* Above: *The Duke and Duchess of York at the National Eisteddfod in Swansea in 1926.*

Top: *After the birth of Princess Elizabeth the Yorks were obliged to go on a world tour which was to prove a conspicuous success. The Duke and Duchess opening the Federal Parliament in Canberra – the Duke's first major test in public duty.* Above: *During the stop in Fiji in February 1927, Ratu Pope E. Seniloli, the grandson of King Cakodau, presented the Duke with a 'tabua', a whale's tooth, a symbol of homage and affection.*

The Duke and Duchess of York at the Guildhall in 1927 when the Duke received the Freedom of the City of London. On the right are the Prince of Wales and the Dukes of Kent and Connaught.

of the tour, convinced that it was his wife whom people wanted to see and uncertain that he could carry on without her. Had he not, at Elizabeth's insistence, gone on alone, he might never have discovered that he was a crowd-puller in his own right, and that he was capable of making a coherent, uninterrupted public address without her at his side. When she was well enough to rejoin him, their success was redoubled. 'The Duchess has had a tremendous ovation,' the Governor of South Australia wrote to the King, 'and leaves us with the responsibility of having a whole continent in love with her.'

From Balmoral, on their return, the King made it clear in a note to the Queen with which of their sons he was the better pleased: 'Delighted to have Bertie with me; he came yesterday evening, have had several talks with him and find him very sensible.' And then again the inevitable, ominous afterthought: 'Very different to David.'

Ahead of them now, although they could not know it, were the most contented five years of their lives. They were able to lay the foundations of a devotedly happy family life; their schedules were busy, but not yet daunting; and the Duchess of

York made it her mission, in the midst of her own ever-busier public routine, to devote herself to the care and support of her husband. She did so with uncanny psychological skill.

Too many accounts of their lives suggest that the relationship was really rather one-sided; that Elizabeth was the making of Bertie, but that he had little to offer her. Certainly, without her, it seems unlikely he would have realised in himself the qualities which were to make him a dignified and respected King. But he too, apart from his constant love, was able to give her in return the sustenance she needed to cope with a life which was not as wholly family-oriented as she would have wished, or as her own upbringing had led her to hope. The mutual growth of their relationship has never been more charmingly described than by Lady Cynthia Colville, who paid this tribute to her friend the Duchess of York: 'This was the measure of her greatness as a woman: she drew him out and made him a man so strong that she could lean on him.'

The King showed his approval by conferring her first public honours upon her, including in August 1927 her very own Regiment, the King's Own Yorkshire Light Infantry, of which she became Colonel-in-Chief. It was to prove, of course, the first of many. As were her patronages, which at first centred on hospitals and other welfare institutions, from Dr Barnardo's and the YWCA to the Putney Home for Incurables. The Scotswoman in her was especially moved in 1929, when her husband was invited to be Lord High Commissioner to the Central Assembly of the Church of Scotland.

Thanks to the King's recurring illnesses, and the Prince of Wales's growing waywardness, the Yorks shouldered more than their fair share of public duties – at a time when the Depression, as always during periods of hardship or national emergency, had the nation looking more than ever to the Royal Family for succour and moral support. For these few heady years, however, they were still not allowed to encroach too much on a family life of which, thanks to the famous indiscretions of their governess 'Crawfie', we have a vivid, if saccharine picture. Miss Marion Crawford spent fifteen years as governess to the Yorks' two daughters before publishing the

The Duke and Duchess of York with General Booth of the Salvation Army at Congress Hall, Clapton in February 1928.

book which so upset the royal family. It was not so much the content as the principle to which they objected, for she loyally testified: 'No one ever had employers who interfered so little. I often had the feeling that the Duke and Duchess, most happy in their own married life, were not over-concerned with the higher education of their daughters. They wanted most for them a really happy childhood, with lots of pleasant memories stored up against the days that might come and, later, happy marriages.'

Nothing, we know from Miss Crawford, was allowed to intrude upon two rituals at each end of the day: the ceremonial romping of children on the parental bed each morning, and the high-spirited bathtime which has remained a tradition with the Windsor dynasty and its young to this day. When the Duke expanded the garden of Royal Lodge, at Windsor, from fifteen to ninety acres, the whole family joined in the task of clearing the wilderness. The King and Queen arrived one weekend to be conducted behind the wheelbarrow of a scruffy Princess Elizabeth to a newly planted tree, beneath which was to be found her father wielding a pair of secateurs. The sombre old King laughed, for once, and his Queen laughed with him. They appreciated above all, as ever, the simple verities of family life.

The Duchess of York at a garden party at Glamis Castle with Princess Elizabeth and Princess Margaret (who was born there) in July 1931.

A far cry from the goings-on down the road at Fort Belvedere, where the Prince of Wales was conducting only semi-discreet affairs with older, married women. Most of fashionable society knew of his liaisons with Mrs Dudley Ward and Lady Furness, and soon they were to hear of the arrival in his life of a Mrs Wallis Simpson. Relations with his brother and his happy family, however, grew if anything closer and more cordial now that they were all spending more time down at Windsor. If their parents were away on official duties, reports Crawfie, it was often Edward, Prince of Wales, who would read to the Princesses Elizabeth and Margaret at teatime.

On one such afternoon he excused himself as the Duchess arrived home, with a remark which in retrospect assumes great poignancy: 'You make family life such fun.' But the truth is that the Duchess of York already took a very dim view of the Prince of Wales's private conduct, and of his high-handed attitude to his royal birthright. In her canny way she perhaps already

The Duke and Duchess of York enjoyed a devotedly happy family life together. The Duchess with King George V, Queen Mary, Princess Elizabeth and Princess Margaret . . . and with her family and assorted pets at Royal Lodge, Windsor.

sensed the 'disaster' that was to come. In the years ahead, to be sure, she would reserve a most uncharacteristic hardness of heart for the Duke of Windsor and even more so for his Duchess – never forgiving the dire consequences of their behaviour upon her husband, herself and her happily tranquil family life.

Elizabeth had little in common with her brother-in-law. Both enjoyed a bright social life, but of a very different kind. Not for her the cocktail circuit and the risqué friends. When not immersed in her own cosy domesticity she preferred the company of one friend for tea or a few for a quiet dinner. And these were tastes entirely shared by her husband. 'They tended', wrote Edward in later years, when Duke of Windsor, 'to withdraw from the hurly-burly of life that I relished.'

The heir apparent was still a very dashing, popular figure: his wartime service in France was taken as a sign that his sense of duty would eventually override his evident appetite for the high life. However, when Britain expected Edward, Prince of Wales, to do his duty and find himself a future Queen, he chose rather to launch himself upon the 1930s with an abandoned self-indulgence none of his younger brothers displayed. George, Duke of Kent, married the beautiful Princess Marina of Greece in 1934; Henry, Duke of Gloucester, married Lady Alice Montague-Douglas-Scott the following year. They knew their father did not have long to live – and they also knew, to their collective horror, that David had embarked on a scandalous romance with a married American woman.

In the early hours of 20 January 1936 King George V died, rather sooner than even his doctors had feared. There are those in the Royal Family who believe to this day that distress over his eldest son's liaison with Mrs Simpson hastened his end; the Prince of Wales had brought her, outrageously in the King's eyes, to his Silver Jubilee ball only a few months before. The matter was never discussed between father and son; yet shortly before his death, the King had voiced his fears to his Prime Minister, Stanley Baldwin: 'After I am dead, that boy will ruin himself within twelve months.'

One of the last pleasures of the old King's life was looking through his binoculars from Buckingham Palace to 145

A visit to the Isle of Skye, 1933.

Piccadilly, where little Princess 'Lilibet' would be waiting at the window to wave to him. It was on one such occasion, again with uncanny foresight, that King George V had expressed his last wish: 'I pray to God that my eldest son will never marry and have children, and that nothing will come between Bertie and Lilibet and the throne.'

59

Queen²

ABDICATION

Edward, Prince of Wales, first met Mrs Wallis Simpson at his Windsor retreat, Fort Belvedere, late in 1930. Such a mythology has come to surround this first encounter that doubts have been cast even on their own respective accounts of it. The least likely small-talk to have passed between them, however, is that most often repeated:

The Prince, on realising that Mrs Simpson is an American: 'Do you not miss the comforts of central heating here in England?'

Mrs Simpson: 'I'm sorry, sir, but you have disappointed me. Every American woman who comes to your country is always asked the same question. I had hoped for something more original from the Prince of Wales.'

As Lady Furness, who introduced them (and was herself American-born), points out: 'Had this been true, it would have been not only bad taste but bad manners.' The truth is that Mrs Simpson, an American divorcée newly married to an Englishman, was thrilled to be introduced into princely circles – and as excited as any mere mortal on first catching sight of, let alone meeting, the Royal Family's most glamorous member. Which is probably why neither of them can remember precisely what, if anything, was actually said. To her the Prince was an icon, a face familiar from souvenirs of all shapes and sizes, and it is an amusing truth that most who meet royalty for the first time in this spirit of dazed curiosity cannot remember much of what was said; it is rarely, for sure, whatever they have long been rehearsing. Edward, for his part, was simply meeting a friend of a close friend, and turning on his instinctive charm. They were to meet socially, with increasing regularity, for the best part of three years before anything more than an acquaintanceship developed.

Wallis Warfield, daughter of an old and prosperous Baltimore family, had been born in Pennsylvania on 19 June 1896. When only nineteen she had married an American naval officer, Earl Winfield Spencer Jr – a surprising choice, given her own unconcealed ambition to 'marry money'. Spencer had neither much money nor much prospect of making any; but the young Wallis apparently found him physically attractive, was of a mind to marry ('to get away from her family,' said a friend) and did so impetuously. It did not last long. Spencer turned out to be neurotically jealous; his wife's public vivacity, whether flirtatious or merely high-spirited, soon turned him into an alcoholic, then a sadist (he would lock her in the bathroom, sometimes all night). It is almost laughably ironic, in the light of subsequent events, that when she told her family she wanted a divorce, these proper Baltimore people threw up their hands in horror and asked her to reconsider. Said her Uncle Sol, who cut her off without a penny, 'The Warfields in all their known connections since 1662 have never had a divorce.' What, he demanded, would people think?

People knew just what they thought when Wallis surfaced in England ten years later, now married to the wealthy, bookish and beetle-browed figure of Ernest Simpson, himself half-American (born of an English father and an American mother, he had taken British citizenship) and already once divorced. She was thought, not to put too fine a point on it, pushy. It is a hard-and-fast misconception that the British establishment's aversion to Mrs Simpson was due either to her being an American or to her being divorced. Many English aristocrats had already taken American brides, Nancy Astor and Emerald Cunard being prominent examples; and high society had learnt, since the days of King Edward VII's offstage antics, to tolerate not merely the *droit du seigneur* exercised by a Prince of Wales over other men's wives but the divorces which inevitably resulted. What people disliked about Mrs Simpson was that she didn't know the proper way to behave in polite society. She combined all the worst hallmarks of determined social climbing with a haughty, self-assertive, very unBritish disregard for propriety. By so publicly taking command of her

Above: *Fort Belvedere, his Windsor retreat, where he first met Mrs Wallis Simpson. Their relationship was destined to place the reluctant Yorks irrevocably in the limelight in their stead.*

Right: *King Edward VIII taking the salute at the Trooping the Colour ceremony in June 1936.*

Prince, and behaving with scant respect towards other members of his family, she committed a social crime much more dastardly than possessing merely the wrong citizenship or marital status.

This is not to suggest that she would have been acceptable as Queen; that was not, as yet, the issue. It is simply to stress that there was widespread anxiety about the Prince of Wales's relationship with Mrs Simpson long before it became clear that King George V was dying. The tragedy of what followed is that no one – least of all his father – tried to do anything about it until, suddenly, it was too late.

It was early in 1934 that the Prince realised he was in love with Mrs Simpson, and late the following year that he must marry her, regardless of the consequences. In his memoirs the Duke of Windsor pleaded with posterity that he would have confided in his parents, sought their guidance, had not 1935 been the year of his father's Silver Jubilee, with unusually heavy public duties already aggravating the King's poor health. It is questionable whether this particular father and son could have discussed such a matter constructively, if at all. What is revealing is the Duke's confession that he was contemplating the marriage, resigned to the fact that it would probably put his brother on the throne, fully a year before it actually did so. And he had never breathed a word to anyone, least of all poor Bertie.

The Prince of Wales's brother and his wife were innocently living out those happy family years, years of growing public popularity, oblivious to the gathering drama elsewhere. The suddenness of George V's death, almost as soon as his Jubilee Year was over, had in itself helped fulfil the King's dying prayer that 'nothing will come between Bertie and Lilibet and the throne'. Such a fate was emphatically not the wish of Bertie and Elizabeth, let alone their nine-year-old daughter. As Heir Presumptive, however, and brother to a man who showed no immediate intention of settling down to the breeding of heirs, Bertie now had to square up to the uncomfortable fact that he or his elder daughter may one day inherit the Crown. Nevertheless, it is unlikely to have crossed his mind, as he and David joined their two younger brothers to stand ceremonial guard over their father's coffin, that 1936 might turn out to be a year in which Britain had three kings, the last of them himself.

The second, however, was more than aware of the possibility. Later that day, as the new King processed behind his father's body through the streets of London, he caught sight of 'a flash of light dancing along the pavement'. It was the Maltese Cross which surmounted the Imperial Crown; a jolt of the gun-carriage had sent it toppling from the catafalque, down into the gutter outside Simpsons-in-the-Strand. 'I wondered', he said later, 'whether it was a bad omen.'

'Christ!' he was heard to exclaim at the time, 'what will happen next?' The two nearby MPs who reported the remark, Walter Elliott and Bob Boothby, turned to each other and agreed it was 'a fitting motto for the coming reign'. Which was to last just 325 days.

King Edward VIII started innovatively. The very night of his father's death he ordered all the Sandringham clocks, kept half an hour fast by the punctual George V, to be restored to Greenwich Mean Time. He then flew to London – the first flight by a British monarch – to preside over his first Privy Council. That day, as he watched his proclamation ceremony at St James's, he insisted on Mrs Simpson's presence at his side. He then blithely proceeded to cause further offence by receiving overseas Ambassadors *en masse*, rather than individually (as was traditional on the occasion of a new King), and abolishing the wearing of ribbons at the monarch's birthday parade. Those who saw all this as a breath of fresh air were further heartened on St David's Day, 1 March, when a broadcast by the new King to his people marked the first time a British monarch had dispensed with the Royal 'we'. But it also betrayed an interest in trivial, symbolic matters at the expense of weightier ones. By April, Downing Street was horrified to hear that Cabinet papers were being left lying around at Frogmore, open to the perusal of Mrs Simpson and the King's own other guests. Some were never returned; and the rings on those that were appeared to come not from the royal pen, but from the wet bottoms of wineglasses.

Bertie, meanwhile, had been put in charge of cost-cutting at Sandringham, which Edward believed 'a voracious white elephant', eating up a disproportionate share of the royal finances. Elizabeth, who had suffered a long bout of bronchitis throughout the traumatic events of the year thus far, was refused doctors' leave to accompany her husband to so cold a place. She had not really been well enough to attend King George V's funeral, but had insisted on being there to lend support to her grief-stricken mother-in-law, with the result that her illness had since worsened. Though melancholy at his wife's absence, the Duke of York was pleased to have been given the task of sorting out Sandringham – and thus, he thought, protect a home of which he was so fond from the caprices of his brother, who had never cared for it. When, that summer, Edward (or, as some say, Mrs Simpson) unceremoniously dismissed many of the long-serving staff at Balmoral – consulting neither Bertie nor Queen Mary – he was relieved to have saved Sandringham from a similar fate.

On becoming Heir Presumptive, the Duke of York had been promoted to the ranks of Vice-Admiral in the Navy, Air Marshal in the RAF and Lieutenant-General in the Army. His income from the Civil List was doubled to £50,000 a year. In the absence of a Queen Consort, and the continued mourning retreat of Queen Mary, Elizabeth had become ex-officio 'first lady of the land'. By an Order in Council, the names of the Duke and Duchess of York were inserted into the standard prayers for the Royal Family recited each Sunday in churches all over the land. Suddenly, to their unease, the Yorks were conspicuously pre-eminent, second only to the King himself, and publicly senior to the rest of the Royal Family.

Uneasy they may have been, having never sought or desired such pre-eminence, but it perhaps helped them both to wake up to the dangers of what was happening across Windsor Great Park at Fort Belvedere. Hitherto, apparently through some sort of lingering wish-fulfilment, Bertie had turned a foolishly deaf ear to all the gossip from the Fort, and the logical consequences of the worst of it. It was during the summer, for the first time, that the Yorks began to grasp the enormity of what might overcome them, and the growing likelihood of its happening.

They were not among the regular visitors to the Fort, where the King spent more and more of his time. Those who were, however, reported that Mrs Simpson had taken thorough charge of the place, tactlessly forcing change upon royal servants who dated back to Victoria. She had been known to kick the King under the table if she wanted to stop him talking, and was not averse to contradicting him publicly and brusquely. All pretence, as in the past, that she was a 'joint' guest with her husband (albeit a *mari complaisant*) – a straw to which Bertie had clung too long – had been abandoned. Mrs Simpson, here as in the other royal residences, had established herself as the King's official hostess.

The significance of it all seems even to have been lost on them that summer, when the King drove over to Royal Lodge one weekend to show off his new American station wagon – and his companion in the passenger seat. 'It was a pleasant hour', the Duchess of Windsor later recalled, 'but I left with a distinct impression that, while the Duke of York was sold on the American station wagon, the Duchess was not sold on David's other American interest.' She was right. Elizabeth was never to 'receive' Mrs Simpson again, nor, for the rest of her life, to take anything less than a wholly unforgiving attitude. She said nothing as Princess Elizabeth, watching the royal couple drive away in their incongruous transport, asked, 'Mummy, who is *she?*'

In a curious way the Yorks seemed happy to deceive themselves, as if willing the inevitable to keep its distance. For a while our protagonists now move into the wings. They were not privy at the time to the thickening of the plot, for reasons both cruel and kind. They were merely bit players in the drama which would soon propel them to centre-stage. Elizabeth, more than Bertie, would resent this – and resent it for the rest of her life.

Down the road at the Fort, the guests included their ever-vigilant, diary-writing friend Harold Nicolson, to whom daily life at court had now become 'really rather second-rate'. To

J. H. Thomas, the pugnacious union leader who had joined the coalition Cabinet, it spelt disaster. "'Ere we 'ave this obstinate little man with 'is Mrs Simpson,' he told Nicolson. 'Hit won't do, 'arold. I tell you that straight. I know the people of this country. They 'ate 'aving no family life at Court.'

Thomas was not the only politician sensing mortal danger to the throne. The Prime Minister, Stanley Baldwin, though outwardly cordial in his relationship with the King, was privately a very worried man. 'When I was a little boy in Worcestershire, reading history books', he told his private secretary, 'I never thought I should have to interfere between a King and his mistress.' But interfere he would have to – and soon.

Up to now the barons of the British press had ordained a remarkable but mutually agreed silence on this sensational story, which had been appearing for months in newspapers and magazines on the continent and across the Atlantic. Even when the King forsook the royal ritual of summering at Balmoral and took Mrs Simpson on an unbelievably indiscreet Adriatic cruise, the British press refrained from reprinting the lurid coverage of their transatlantic and European cousins. There was the King, his married mistress on his arm, wading ashore shirtless (with pained, pinstriped officials in tow) to lunch with foreign princes and potentates in quayside cafés – and Fleet Street breathed not a word. It could not, to be sure, happen today.

Baldwin knew it could not last much longer. He had hoped that *someone* in the Royal Family – Queen Mary, perhaps, or the Duke of York – might speak to the King upon his return about the impossibility of maintaining this status quo. When David returned on 14 September, however, it was to a private dinner with Queen Mary at which the matter went quite undiscussed. 'Didn't you find it terribly hot?' was about the most trenchant question his arch old mother asked him. 'David got back looking very well,' was all she told even her diary. 'We had a nice talk.'

For their own private reasons, even the most senior members of the Royal Family either could not or would not confront the

King with his own folly. The government, therefore, had to act. On 2 October, nearly a month later, Baldwin sought an audience with his monarch at which he showed him letters he had received from all over the Empire, deploring his relationship with Mrs Simpson, the publicity it had earned everywhere but in Britain, and the constitutional consequences of his apparent wish to marry her. At the time the lady herself had retreated to Suffolk, where she at least had had the discretion to file her divorce proceedings against her husband. Baldwin begged the King to get her to drop the case; the newspapers' right to report it would inevitably open the floodgates of publicity and force the whole issue into the public domain, where they would both lose control of it. The King rather irritably replied that it was not for him to interfere in other people's business. The divorce case must go ahead.

KING'S MOLL RENO'D IN WOLSEY'S HOME TOWN was the headline in one American paper – a classic of the genre – when Mrs Simpson's decree nisi was granted in Ipswich. French sub-editors preferred the more romantic L'AMOUR DE ROI VA BIEN. Still, amazing though it may seem, the British public lived largely in ignorance of the whole business. His family being unwilling, and his government unable, to bring the King to his senses, his private secretary, Major Alexander Hardinge, took his life in his hands with a dramatic, scrupulously worded, private letter which tersely summed up the state of the nation. The silence of the press, he argued from inside knowledge, could not be maintained much longer. The choices were thus bleak: either the King must face the possible resignation of his government – and a general election 'in which Your Majesty's personal affairs would be the chief issue' – or Mrs Simpson must be sent abroad *'without further delay'*. It was the only way to buy time for a considered decision and to avoid 'the damage which would inevitably be done to the Crown – the cornerstone on which the whole Empire rests'.

There followed a postscript detailing where Major Hardinge would be the next day (shooting near High Wycombe) should the King have need of his services. But rather than taking this painfully honest document in the spirit in which it was sent,

Edward was apparently 'shocked and angered' by it. From that moment on, he had no further dealings with the loyal Major Hardinge.

However, the document did, at least, make him realise the game was up. Whether or not he must abandon his lingering hopes of marrying Mrs Simpson *and* remaining King – even if the marriage were, as Lord Rothermere suggested, a morganatic one – it was time to make his intentions clear to the Prime Minister, if no one else. Edward summoned Baldwin two days later and told him categorically that he proposed to marry Mrs Simpson as soon as she was legally free. He hoped to do so as King; but if the Government remained irrevocably opposed, he would abdicate.

Baldwin, who had not expected such single-mindedness, was stunned into silence. 'Sir,' he said, 'this is most grievous news, and it is impossible for me to make any comment on it today.' Back at Downing Street he decided to sleep on it. 'I have heard such things from my King tonight as I never thought to hear,' he told his Chief Whip. 'I am going to my bed.'

The King, by contrast, sensed a sudden, almost heady mood of release. The same evening, he went to tell Queen Mary of his unshakeable resolve. And next day he told his brother Bertie, hitherto wholly uninvolved and unconsulted in a matter which had so direct and drastic a bearing on his own future. He and Elizabeth went off to Edinburgh, where he was to be installed as Grand Master Mason of Scotland, in a state of utter dejection. 'I feel', he told his private secretary, 'like the proverbial sheep being led to the slaughter.'

Still there were those who thought abdication could be avoided. Winston Churchill, in his romantic way, made a plea for 'time and patience'. Other, more outlandish solutions were canvassed while still the press kept its corporate finger in the dyke. Then came the event which, in its unlikely way, at last pulled that finger out.

On Tuesday 1 December the Bishop of Bradford, meaning to make a veiled but stern criticism of the King's infrequent churchgoing, told his Diocesan Conference: 'I commend the King to God's grace – for the King is a man like ourselves. We

CLOSING CITY PRICES

FINAL NIGHT

Evening Standard

No. 35,036   LONDON, THURSDAY, DECEMBER 10, 1936   ONE PENNY

THE KING ABDICATES
Duke of York Monarch

THE following message from his Majesty King Edward VIII. was read in the House of Commons this afternoon by the Speaker:

AFTER LONG AND ANXIOUS CONSIDERATION I HAVE DETERMINED TO RENOUNCE THE THRONE TO WHICH I SUCCEEDED ON THE DEATH OF MY FATHER, AND I AM COMMUNICATING THIS, MY FINAL AND IRREVOCABLE DECISION.

REALISING AS I DO THE GRAVITY OF THIS STEP, I CAN ONLY HOPE THAT I SHALL HAVE THE UNDERSTANDING OF MY PEOPLES IN THE DECISION I HAVE TAKEN AND THE REASONS WHICH HAVE LED ME TO TAKE IT.

I WILL NOT ENTER NOW INTO MY PRIVATE FEELINGS, BUT I WOULD BEG THAT IT SHOULD BE REMEMBERED THAT THE BURDEN WHICH CONSTANTLY RESTS UPON THE SHOULDERS OF A SOVEREIGN IS SO HEAVY THAT IT CAN ONLY BE BORNE IN CIRCUMSTANCES DIFFERENT FROM THOSE IN WHICH I NOW FIND MYSELF.

I CONCEIVE THAT I AM NOT OVERLOOKING THE DUTY THAT RESTS ON ME TO PLACE IN THE FOREFRONT THE PUBLIC INTERESTS WHEN I DECLARE THAT I AM CONSCIOUS THAT I CAN NO LONGER DISCHARGE THIS HEAVY TASK WITH EFFICIENCY OR WITH SATISFACTION TO MYSELF.

I HAVE ACCORDINGLY THIS MORNING EXECUTED AN INSTRUMENT OF ABDICATION IN THE TERMS FOLLOWING :—

I, EDWARD VIII. OF GREAT BRITAIN, IRELAND, AND THE BRITISH DOMINIONS BEYOND THE SEAS, KING, EMPEROR OF INDIA, DO HEREBY DECLARE MY IRREVOCABLE DETERMINATION TO RENOUNCE THE THRONE FOR MYSELF AND FOR MY DESCENDANTS, AND MY DESIRE THAT EFFECT SHOULD BE GIVEN TO THIS INSTRUMENT OF ABDICATION IMMEDIATELY.

IN TOKEN WHEREOF I HAVE HEREUNTO SET MY HAND THIS TENTH DAY OF DECEMBER, NINETEEN HUNDRED AND THIRTY-SIX IN THE PRESENCE OF THE WITNESSES WHOSE SIGNATURES ARE SUBSCRIBED.

EDWARD R.I.

MY EXECUTION OF THIS INSTRUMENT HAS BEEN WITNESSED BY MY THREE BROTHERS, THEIR ROYAL HIGHNESSES THE DUKE OF YORK, THE DUKE OF GLOUCESTER, AND THE DUKE OF KENT.

I DEEPLY APPRECIATE THE SPIRIT WHICH HAS ACTUATED THE APPEALS WHICH HAVE BEEN MADE TO ME TO TAKE A DIFFERENT DECISION, AND I HAVE, BEFORE REACHING MY FINAL DETERMINATION, MOST FULLY PONDERED OVER THEM.

BUT MY MIND IS MADE UP.

MOREOVER, FURTHER DELAY CANNOT BUT BE MOST INJURIOUS TO THE PEOPLES WHOM I HAVE TRIED TO SERVE AS PRINCE OF WALES AND AS KING, AND WHOSE FUTURE HAPPINESS AND PROSPERITY ARE THE CONSTANT WISH OF MY HEART.

I TAKE LEAVE OF THEM IN THE CONFIDENT HOPE THAT THE COURSE WHICH I HAVE THOUGHT IT RIGHT TO FOLLOW IS THAT WHICH IS BEST FOR THE STABILITY OF THE THRONE AND EMPIRE AND THE HAPPINESS OF MY PEOPLES.

I AM DEEPLY SENSIBLE OF THE CONSIDERATION WHICH THEY HAVE ALWAYS EXTENDED TO ME BOTH BEFORE AND AFTER MY ACCESSION TO THE THRONE, AND WHICH I KNOW THEY WILL EXTEND IN FULL MEASURE TO MY SUCCESSOR.

I AM MOST ANXIOUS THAT THERE SHOULD BE NO DELAY OF ANY KIND IN GIVING EFFECT TO THE INSTRUMENT WHICH I HAVE EXECUTED, AND THAT ALL NECESSARY STEPS SHOULD BE TAKEN IMMEDIATELY TO SECURE THAT MY LAWFUL SUCCESSOR, MY BROTHER, HIS ROYAL HIGHNESS THE DUKE OF YORK, SHOULD ASCEND THE THRONE.

EDWARD R.I.

The Prime Minister told the House how King Edward came to his decision—See Page Two

The Abdication Speech, 10 December 1936.

hope that he is aware of his need. Some of us wish that he gave more positive signs of his awareness.' Jumping to the wrong conclusions, the Yorkshire press reported the Bishop's remarks as breaking the Establishment silence on the King's relationship with Mrs Simpson. The national press could not but pick up where the provincials had left off, and the floodgates were opened. Bertie and Elizabeth were horrified, on their return from Scotland that Thursday, to see London newspaper placards proclaiming THE KING'S MARRIAGE.

73

Now, as Mrs Simpson was spirited out of the country and the crisis could be put off no longer, the Duke of York's stammer ('God's curse upon me', he called it) returned with a vengeance. At 145 Piccadilly the informal Yorks, embarrassed by stiff protocol, had always shrugged off the need for sentries on the door, but armed guards were now required to keep the volatile crowds at bay, once news of the King's long-secret romance had become public. It was thought prudent to inspire one or two newspaper articles about 'Our future Queen?', to divert attention from the real matter of the moment, so the Duchess of York was forced to tolerate the kind of publicity she had always shunned for her children. A Post Office engineer who had spanked Princess Elizabeth for rifling in his toolbag, and thought her mother seemed 'rather pleased', became a national celebrity.

Such trivia only added salt to the Yorks' wounds. Their greatest grievance, which still smarts with the Queen Mother to this day, was that Bertie was so little involved or consulted in the to-ings and fro-ings between King, Prime Minister and intermediaries during Edward's days of decision in the autumn of 1936. Even in the fateful December week which ended it all, the Duke made appointments to see his brother only with the greatest difficulty, and even then most of them were cancelled without explanation at the last minute. The one saving grace is that there were hidden reasons.

Thanks to his official biographer, Sir John Wheeler-Bennett, we have King George VI's own handwritten account of his side of the events leading up to his reluctant assumption of that title.

On the evening of Thursday 3 December, Bertie noted in his diary a 'dreadful announcement' to the family by his brother: 'David said to Queen Mary that he could not live alone as King and must marry Mrs S———.' [He could never bring himself, whether in conversation or the privacy of his diary, to mention Mrs Simpson's name.] The King's last words that night were to ask Bertie to come and see him at Fort Belvedere, his Windsor home, the next morning. But again the appointment was cancelled. Saturday . . . Sunday . . . Monday . . . appointments were made, appointments were cancelled. Often

The least security-conscious of people, the Yorks were nevertheless obliged to have armed sentries on guard outside their home, 145 Piccadilly during the Abdication crisis.

the King would not even come to the phone. All weekend the Yorks waited – he constantly telephoning his brother and constantly being stalled, she relapsing into a particularly severe version of her annual bout of flu.

Finally, on the Monday evening, after a devastating series of rebuffs, the King telephoned his brother at 6.50 pm to say, 'Come and see me after dinner.' *After* dinner? No, replied Bertie, at last showing some resolve, I'm coming at once.

'I was with him at 7.00 pm. The awful & ghastly suspense of waiting was over. I found him pacing up & down the room, and he told me his decision that he would go. I went back to Royal Lodge for dinner & returned to the Fort later. I felt having once got there I was not going to leave. As he is my eldest brother I had to be there to try & help him in his hour of need. I went back to London that night with my wife.'

Why had Bertie been so painfully excluded from the deliberations of that long and dramatic weekend? It seems likely that his elder brother, as his own hopes and certainties came and went almost as frequently as the Prime Minister, was being cruel only to be kind.

It was a time of mounting political anxiety in Europe. If Britain were to have a new King, at a time of constitutional crisis, then Britain deserved the best available candidate. The plain fact is that both King and Government were considering bypassing the ill-at-ease, stammering Duke of York – and Harry, Duke of Gloucester, a rather dim career soldier none too devoted to what he called 'princing about' – and offering the throne to their youngest brother George, Duke of Kent, a dashing and much more confident 34-year-old with the added advantage of a male heir. There is nothing in the British constitution to specify that after an abdication, and especially in the absence of an heir apparent, the throne must pass to the

While King Edward VIII deliberated on his future, there was much to-ing and fro-ing at Number 10, Downing Street. Top: *The Attorney-General, Walter Monckton, and* (left) *the Archbishop of Canterbury, Cosmo Lang, were among those who called on the Prime Minister, Stanley Baldwin,* (right) *during the Abdication crisis.*

76

next in the line of succession. It is merely customary, after the death of one monarch, for the heir presumptive to succeed. Abdication, by contrast, requires an act of parliament, in which event it is up to parliament to specify the succession.

The implications are stunning. The Duke of Kent, as events transpired, was to be killed on active service in 1942; but had he become King in 1936 he would presumably not have been allowed to serve. Either way, the present Duke of Kent would now have been King, and the Queen merely a princess royal.

Not surprisingly, it is a subject you raise in royal circles today at your peril. Mere political developments are revealed after thirty years when the relevant Cabinet papers become available at the Public Records Office; anything pertaining to the royal family, however, is still subject to a 100-year embargo. So even when future historians, fifty years from now, finally dig through the relevant archives, they may well find no record of what happened. They already have the consolation of knowing, as neither King nor Cabinet did at that time, that the Duke of Kent was by then already seriously addicted to what would now be called 'heavy' drugs, and that his succession would thus have been a disaster.

Beyond surmise, on the available facts, is the evidence that the proven virtues of his wife helped restore the balance in the Duke of York's favour. Bertie's record of poor health told against him, as did his inexperience in affairs of state, his newly returned public nervousness (as symbolised by his stammer) and perhaps above all his unconcealed reluctance to take on the job. But Elizabeth now had thirteen years of royal success behind her. She was immensely popular with the public; she had worked hard and effectively in her chosen spheres of royal patronage; she had left a lasting impression upon the Empire and Dominions (a vociferous group in the anti-Simpson faction); she was known by church leaders to be devoutly religious; and she had won the heart of every politician who had met her. Bertie might be a bit of a risk as King, but she was certain to be the perfect Consort.

So Prince Albert, in the end, it would be. All these deliberations, and indeed the decision, had taken place not merely without his participation but without his knowledge. It is far from certain how much he ever knew of them. It was a singular act of kindness on the part of his brother – literally singular, given the otherwise grievous burden he was imposing on him – to attempt to ensure that Bertie would never know the extent to which his abilities had been so doubted. All the King revealed, when he finally saw his brother that Monday evening, was that he had decided to 'go'.

Next day, by the Duke of York's own account, 'I broke down and sobbed like a child.' Another forty-eight hours and there dawned 'that dreadful day', Friday 11 December, which brought a distressingly deadpan telegram from his brother in Boulogne, en route to Austria: HAD A GOOD CROSSING. HOPE ELIZABETH BETTER. BEST LOVE AND BEST OF LUCK TO YOU BOTH. DAVID. Bertie still could not get over the fact that David's last act, as they parted as freemasons at Windsor, was to bow to him.

The 'unthinkable' had happened. The Duke and Duchess of York were King and Queen. 'If someone should come through on the telephone,' Bertie asked Elizabeth over lunch, 'who should I say I am?'

This lovely portrait of the Duchess of York and her two daughters was taken in December 1936, the month of the Abdication which was to alter the family's lives forever.

QUEEN

'I can hardly now believe that we have been called to this tremendous task,' the new Queen wrote to the Archbishop of Canterbury, Cosmo Lang. 'And the curious thing is that we are not afraid. I feel that God has enabled us to face the situation calmly.'

Elizabeth was a good deal calmer than her husband. 'Dickie, this is absolutely terrible,' Bertie confided to his cousin and friend Lord Mountbatten. 'I'm quite unprepared for it. David has been trained for this all his life. I've never even seen a State paper. I'm only a Naval officer – it's the only thing I know about.' Mountbatten, himself of course a Navy man, replied: 'There is no finer training for a King.' And Elizabeth, he went on, would make a 'perfect' Queen.

Even the outgoing King, in his famous farewell radio broadcast from Windsor Castle, had acknowledged the advantages Elizabeth conferred on his brother. 'He has one matchless blessing, enjoyed by so many of you and not bestowed on me – a happy home with his wife and children.' The new King, for his part, paid due tribute to his Consort on his first full day as monarch, addressing a loyal if shell-shocked gathering of his Privy Council: 'With my wife and helpmeet by my side, I take up the heavy burden which lies before me.'

His wife and helpmeet, if truth be known, was equally appalled by the 'awful' fate which had befallen them; but she was much better equipped to cope with it. As despatch boxes full of Cabinet papers began to flow into his office, George VI sorely regretted his father's insistence on refusing him access to these and other aspects of the constitutional process. At first the new King was unable to conceal from his intimates the full extent of his bewilderment. He passed from a state of shock through one of numbness to sheer emotional exhaustion. But with the help of his single-minded wife, he soon began to tap reserves of strength which perhaps only such a crisis could have revealed.

The gravity of that crisis is not to be underestimated. In those first few, unreal days of the new reign, there was a distinct possibility (as the King himself put it privately) that the whole 'fabric' of the monarchy might 'crumble'. The British people were still torn about the fate of their last, all too short-lived King; the news of his dilemma had burst upon them with such suddenness that his fate had been resolved before public opinion had had a chance to make itself felt. In the absence of much clear information, there were many who believed – as the ex-King himself eventually came to – that sinister plots by Baldwin and others had hounded him from the throne. And there was widespread doubt whether his diffident, stammering brother was really up to the job. It had certainly been ill-advised of him to be quite so open about his reluctance to succeed.

As the facts of the abdication gradually became known, there set in a public disenchantment with the conduct of King Edward VIII from which his successor benefited personally, but the institution of monarchy did not. Even a staunch Conservative MP, Sir Arnold Wilson, feared that fully 100 members of the House of Commons, given the chance, would vote for the abolition of the monarchy in favour of a republic. And some leading republicans were seizing the hour to create that chance.

During the debate on the Abdication Bill, James Maxton MP thundered that 'the Humpty Dumpty of royalty' had fallen from the wall, and no power could put him back again. 'We are doing a wrong and foolish thing,' declared Maxton, a radical Labour Member but a popular and respected parliamentarian, 'if we do not seize the opportunity of establishing in our land a completely democratic form of government, which does away with our monarchical institutions and the hereditary principle.'

The vote went heavily in the Government's favour; but it remains an indication of the House's mood that such sentiments were heard there at all. They could scarcely be voiced today. Equally striking, fifty years on, is the evidence of a December 1936 newspaper poll that almost half the respondents favoured abolition.

The royal family is still haunted by the memory of this, the moment the British constitutional monarchy was brought to its knees. To this day, abdication remains a dirty word in royal circles. She can joke about it – 'We'll go quietly,' she once said to an avowed republican – but Queen Elizabeth II in fact believes history will regard her central achievement as having rebuilt the monarchy on the firm foundations laid by her father. A mere half-century on, as Britain and the Commonwealth warms to the next royal generation now carefully being coaxed to the front of the stage, the institution of monarchy is as popular and secure as it has ever been – as witnessed by the remarkable displays of public affection during the Queen's Silver Jubilee in 1977 and the Prince of Wales's wedding four years later.

In 1936, however, Elizabeth II was just a ten-year-old child, the daughter of parents newly bowed down by heavy, unsought responsibilities. With the European crisis worsening, it was an unhappy time indeed for basic British institutions to be shaken to their constitutional core. And it augured well for the King's uncertain future that, sensing this, he saw a chance to make a very personal contribution towards healing the nation's wounds.

On the very first evening of his reign, Bertie had already shown unexpected political skills when confronted with the problem of what his brother should now be called. Sir John Reith, Director General of the BBC, who was to announce the ex-King's farewell broadcast from Windsor, proposed to introduce him as Mr Edward Windsor. 'This is quite wrong,' the new King snapped at his assembled protocol experts, who confessed themselves unable to come up with an acceptable alternative. He would be announced tonight, the King ordered, as Prince Edward; and henceforth he would be formally known as His Royal Highness The Duke of Windsor.

Bertie had worked it all out. His brother had been born the

son of a Duke and was therefore entitled to the rank of prince. More important, the rank of plain Mr would enable him, should he so choose, to return to Britain and stand for parliament (agreed by all present to be an 'undesirable' possibility). As a Duke, he would be able to speak freely on political subjects in the House of Lords; but as a royal Duke – in other words, as a Royal Highness – he would not.

Now the new King showed equal canniness in the choice of his own public name. Rather than use the one by which he was known, thus granting Queen Victoria's dearest posthumous wish by becoming King Albert I, King George VI shrewdly chose so to style himself in the interests of continuity and stability. For the same reason, when asked if he wished to wait the customary year before being crowned, he opted for the imminent date already scheduled for his brother's coronation. The message he sent to the Lord Chamberlain's office was a laconic 'Same date, different King.'

Bertie's attitude to his brother's conduct was still more one of blank astonishment than of pained or angry recrimination. The new Queen, however, took a wholly unforgiving attitude to the conduct of her brother-in-law and 'that woman'. In Edward's brief year as King she had been particularly stung to have been received at Balmoral by Mrs Simpson – unforgivably, in her view, taking over Queen Mary's role as the King's hostess. The memory rankled, a symbol of everything Elizabeth couldn't stand about the *arriviste* American divorcée. Neither as Queen, nor since as Queen Mother, has she ever been willing to receive the Duchess. Only the express (and firmly stated) wish of her daughter the Queen persuaded her to be seen, let alone photographed, anywhere near her at the few royal occasions attended by this royal pariah – notably the Duke's funeral in 1972. To this day the Queen Mother is capable of referring in private to the Duchess of Windsor as 'the woman who killed my husband'.

In the early days after the abdication, it was the Queen who had to coax her husband into taking a firm line with the Duke on several causes of embarrassment between brother and brother, King and ex-King. The most awkward was the difficulty of persuading the ex-King that he no longer had a say in the running of the monarchy – or the country. In his first few weeks on the throne Bertie, who had always adored and admired his elder brother, was subjected to a torrent of phone calls from a series of temporary homes on the continent, offering advice about this and that, ruminating on the political situation, pleading about the vexed question of his wife's rank. Surely, once they were married, she would be entitled to be addressed as a Royal Highness?

One evening there was a message for the King to call his brother in Austria. He did so, only to be told by a switchboard operator that the Duke of Windsor was half-way through an enjoyable dinner; he would have to call back later. If Bertie was hurt, Elizabeth was outraged. She would not have her brother-in-law using his own self-confidence to undermine her husband's. It would have to stop. The Palace switchboard was told, to general embarrassment, that the Duke was no longer to be put through to the King; and Walter Monckton, who had replaced Hardinge as his representative throughout the abdication crisis, was despatched to France to tell the Duke to desist. He, for his part, supposed the message not really to originate from his brother but from his tougher-minded sister-in-law.

The Queen Mother's harsh attitude to the Duke, and even more so to Mrs Simpson, is sometimes portrayed as the sole blot on her escutcheon. With the benefit of hindsight most Britons today would surely feel fond enough of this venerable royal figure to sympathise – even if she carried her resentment to an inflexible extreme which is markedly out of character. But in 1936 there was scant time for recrimination. It was a moment for retrenchment, for finding a formula which would restore the monarchy's tarnished reputation with its people, and keeping republican sentiments – let alone the pro-Windsor proponents of a 'King's Party' – at bay.

In naming himself after his father, King George VI was quite consciously returning to the traditional values and aspirations of King George V's reign. Now, as he and his wife enjoyed a brief respite over Christmas at Sandringham – at their happiest, as always, in the bosom of their family – they less consciously struck a style which would serve their purposes more eloquently than could any cruder, contrived piece of public relations in the difficult years ahead.

George VI's official biographer has listed what he saw as the outstanding qualities the King brought to his office: 'Common sense and human understanding, great personal integrity, combined with a deep humility, a keen sense of public service, moral and physical courage above the ordinary, and a sincere recognition of dependence upon the grace and guidance of Almighty God.' These were naturally the qualities which also informed the new monarch's private life. And it was through his wife and children, through the tangible public relief that a decent, happy, down-to-earth, almost ordinary family had inherited the throne, that these qualities began to win him the people's hearts and minds.

There was a great sympathy with Elizabeth's evident determination to minimise the effect of their new eminence upon her family's visibly happy private life, while dedicating herself and her children to public service. Shrewdly, perhaps instinctively, she recognised (like the wily J. H. Thomas) that most Britons look to royalty as a symbol of family life at its most tranquil, contented and traditional. Even the Duke of Windsor, in his memoirs, acknowledged this truth when paying tribute to his father: 'The King himself, in the role of the bearded paterfamilias, his devoted and queenly wife, their four grown sons and a daughter, not to mention the rising generation of grandchildren – he transformed the Crown as personified by the royal family into a model of the traditional family virtues...'

By conspicuously upholding the moral norms of family living, the First Family of the land was performing its most important, quasi-religious function – as indeed holds true to this day. The Princesses Elizabeth and Margaret, hitherto carefully screened from publicity, emerged to most Britons as an unexpected bonus about this reluctant King and his more relaxed, ever-smiling wife. In this more than anything else, as they had hoped, Bertie and Elizabeth reawakened affectionate public memories of the mood of his father's reign. Even the G.R.I. of his official signature, his friend and adviser Lord Wigram was touched to note, was almost indistinguishable from that of King George V.

Much of the early part of the New Year was spent preparing for the ordeal of their coronation, an awesome ceremony which both found themselves dreading. The fact that they were devoutly religious people eased their discussions with the Archbishop of Canterbury; all three were concerned that the occasion be more than ever a showpiece for the religious aspects of monarchy. Even today, the British people tend, to underestimate the significance attached by the senior members of the royal family to the sacred nature of the Crown; the fate to which they are born, they are brought up to believe, amounts to a religious duty. In 1936, as the head of a family dedicated to the service of the nation, King George VI felt a profound sense of proxy guilt for what he regarded as a gross dereliction of duty by his brother. The nation, the Commonwealth, the Dominions had been badly let down. 'I am new to the job', the King wrote to his Prime Minister, Baldwin, 'but I hope that time will be allowed to me to make amends for what has happened.'

The King, after all, was not merely the titular head of the Church of England; he was, in the words of Walter Bagehot, 'the head of our morality'. With this symbolic role in mind, he wanted the people to be able to feel involved in the Coronation service as never before. The King himself overrode the opposition of some senior churchmen to the BBC's plans to broadcast the service – a telling contrast to his meek surrender at the time of his wedding service fourteen years before. He felt deep anxiety about successfully negotiating the spoken parts of the service before an audience of so many millions, but was otherwise in excellent health and determined, optimistic mood.

It was therefore doubly unfair that the run-up to the Coronation saw a wave of malicious gossip about his health and abilities, much of it fed by the pro-Windsor press of Lord Beaverbrook. The fact that he had declined to attend the traditional Indian Durbar – in truth because he had felt it unwise to leave the country for so long in the first year of his reign, especially given a change of government – was used to suggest that the King was in even weaker physical condition than was generally supposed. The order of the Coronation service had been much changed, in an earnest attempt by both King and Archbishop to reinforce its spiritual significance; as word of this got about, it was suggested that it had been shortened merely to enable him to get through it without any embarrassments. Popular opinion drifted in the dangerous direction that he was an ailing puppet of the government, a 'rubber-stamp King' at a time when Britain needed a resolute monarch to help it face the growing likelihood of war in Europe. There was very little either King or Government could do about this uncomfortable turn of events – made worse by a tactless broadcast by the Archbishop of Canterbury, which by trying to make sympathetic noises about his speech defect succeeded only in drawing more attention to it.

Other loyalists leapt to the rescue with public speeches which amounted, in the most bizarre way, to character references for the King – many, like the Archbishop's, only adding fuel to the flames. Elizabeth told Bertie that only a public display of his growing self-confidence could save the day. So immense importance was suddenly attached to a speech he was due to make on St George's Day, less than a month before the Coronation. Hours each day were spent under Lionel Logue's tutelage, practising from drafts of the text and repeating the breathing exercise which had worked such wonders. In the event, the speech passed off so well that Logue had the satisfaction of hearing someone near him in the audience say to his wife: 'Didn't the Archbishop say this man had a speech defect, my dear?' To which she replied: 'You shouldn't believe all you hear, dear, not even from Archbishops.'

And so it came to pass, on 12 May 1937, fourteen years after her wedding, that the reluctant royal duchess found herself back in Westminster Abbey, to be crowned an even more reluctant Queen. A coronation, whatever the circumstances, is always a psychologically powerful moment of rededication for

At the Coronation of King George VI in Westminster Abbey on 14 May 1939 there was also a crown for Queen Elizabeth – and for the two princesses, who appeared on the balcony of Buckingham Palace.

the nation at large, and particularly so for the two figures at the centre of its awesome ceremonial. As the Archbishop of Canterbury testified, the experience left Bertie and Elizabeth both stirred and inspired, if still haunted by the circumstances which now found them on those golden thrones in Westminster Abbey.

Around the country it was a day of mixed emotions. The nation was all too aware that this was the date originally fixed for the coronation of King Edward VIII; all the souvenirs had already been marketed (and to this day Edward VIII coronation mugs have a special collectors' value). In his exile abroad, moreover, the discredited ex-King remained a source of powerful fascination to his former subjects. Now, hard upon the heels of one King's coronation, was to follow his predecessor's marriage in France. The date Edward chose, to the renewed consternation of his mother, Queen Mary, was 3 June, the birthday of his late father, King George V.

It was the new King George himself who ruled that the Duchess of Windsor was *not* to enjoy the style and dignity of Royal Highness – news which would quite spoil his brother's wedding day. It was, however, the eternal emissary Walter Monckton who had to deliver the royal kidney-punch as he arrived, the sole representative of the British Establishment, to attend the wedding at the Château de Candé, near Tours. Along with messages of goodwill from the Duke's brother, Monckton handed over Letters Patent from King George VI in which his Majesty was 'pleased to declare that the Duke of Windsor shall, notwithstanding his act of Abdication . . . be entitled to hold and enjoy *for himself only* the style and attribute of Royal Highness, so however that his wife and descendants, if any, shall *not* hold the said title or attribute.' [My italics]

It was, cursed the Duke, a 'damnable' wedding present. Thus began a debate which still remains unresolved, on both the morality and the humanity of the King's decision. Its legality, given that the situation was without precedent and that the rank of Royal Highness is entirely within the King's gift, was not in question. But if Edward had forsaken his throne to marry a woman unacceptable as Queen, should he not have

After the Coronation ceremony the two princesses posed with their parents for official Coronation portraits.

had the consolation prize of sharing with her the rank he retained in lieu? King George VI thought not, for two reasons.

First, he believed quite simply that if Mrs Simpson had proved unacceptable as Queen, she was for the same reasons unacceptable as a Royal Highness. Secondly, and more pragmatically, he simply did not believe the marriage would last. Like his mother Queen Mary, Bertie still found himself unable to believe his brother's priorities. 'It seemed inconceivable to those who made such sacrifices during the war', Queen Mary wrote to the exiled Duke, 'that you, as their King, refused a lesser sacrifice.' These were King George VI's sentiments entirely. He believed that Mrs Simpson had temporarily 'deranged' his brother, and feared the consequences of awarding the rank of HRH to a woman who already had three living husbands and may before too long have yet more. As he wrote to Baldwin: 'Once a person has become a Royal Highness, there is no means of depriving her of the title.'

Baldwin was impressed. In this tricky matter at least, the new King was proving himself more decisive than anyone had reason to hope. He had also himself dealt quickly and efficiently with such other thorny questions as his brother's life tenancy of the privately owned royal residences, Sandringham and Balmoral. George VI, while personally settling his brother's title and rank, also sorted out a very generous financial settlement, which Baldwin's Cabinet was only too happy to approve. Soon after the Coronation, Baldwin felt sufficient confidence in the status quo to tender his long postponed resignation as Prime Minister.

'He's coming on magnificently,' Ramsay MacDonald told the Queen, somewhat patronisingly, as they both watched George VI speaking at a public function. 'And how am I doing?' she inquired of the former Prime Minister with the sweetest of smiles. 'Oh, you . . .!' said MacDonald, making her realise that to him, as to Baldwin, her success had never been in doubt.

As Queen Consort, Elizabeth was now addressed as 'Your Majesty' and had her own flag and coat-of-arms, as well as a greatly enlarged staff financed out of the £40,000 a year she now received in her own right from the Civil List. Just as her children had got used to calling themselves York – 'I'd only just learnt how to spell it,' complained Princess Margaret Rose – they now had no surname at all.

While offering Bertie all the support he sought in matters constitutional, Elizabeth had found there was even more to be getting on with on the domestic front. There were her brother-in-law's heedless administrative changes at all the royal palaces (except, thanks to Bertie, Sandringham) to set to rights. Above all there was their main home, Buckingham Palace – which had a cold, neglected air about it even after so short and absent a reign – to make into a more cheerful place. It was characteristic that her first act on moving in was to abolish the tradition whereby the sovereign's offspring bowed or curtsied to him each day.

Buckingham Palace has never been the royal family's favourite home. The Duke of Windsor called it 'a sepulchre'; that 'vast building with its stately rooms and endless corridors and passages', he wrote, 'seemed pervaded by a curious musty smell . . . I was never happy there.' Elizabeth set determinedly about the difficult task of making the palace a home as well as an office, winning round staff who were at first a little wary of the reputedly dull Yorks after the provenly fun-loving Windsors. The imperious style of Mrs Simpson was quickly forgotten as the homely, down-to-earth new Queen took personal charge of table settings, flower arrangements and the decor of the rooms both private and public. To her guests, many making a none too subtle switch of allegiances now that the pendulum had swung the Yorks' way, she was a faultless hostess. The ever vigilant Harold Nicolson, who managed to keep a foot in each camp, visiting the Windsors in France while still being received at court, said of one dinner party at Windsor: 'I cannot tell you how superb she was. What astonished me is how the King has changed. He is now like his brother. He was so gay and she so calm . . . I cannot help feeling what a mess poor Mrs Simpson would have made of the occasion. It demonstrates to us more than anything else how wholly impossible that marriage would have been.'

Over those first twelve months of George VI's reign the abdication, thanks as much as anything else to the conspiracy of silence among the British press, soon proved a nine-day wonder. With the ex-King out of sight and ever more out of mind, the crisis he had created for the monarchy evaporated almost as swiftly as it had burst upon the national consciousness.

By 10 December 1937, the first anniversary of George VI's accession, the Archbishop of Canterbury was able to write to the King: 'It falls to me, I suppose, as much as to any public man, to meet all sorts and conditions of people, and to learn what is in their minds. I find everywhere the same testimony to the impression which Your Majesty and the Queen have made upon your people during the first year of your reign. At first the feeling was one of sympathy and hope. Now it is one of admiration and confidence.'

The following year was to see these qualities emerge ever more strongly in both King and Queen, against the darkening backdrop of the inevitable drift towards war. In July the

Queen Elizabeth and Queen Mary with the two princesses – a Guide and a Brownie – in the Quadrangle of Windsor Castle during a Girl Guide rally in 1938.

Queen's dearly loved mother, Lady Strathmore, died after a long illness. Family mourning caused the postponement of a state visit to France, but personal grief eventually had to take second place to greater anxieties as Hitler's remorseless progress across Europe continued. The royal couple returned from a triumphant success in Paris to a London where trenches were being dug, sandbags and gasmasks distributed and children evacuated to the countryside. Despite the phoney delay won by Chamberlain at Munich, war could now only be a matter of time.

Meanwhile, the Duke and Duchess of Windsor continued to cause grievous embarrassment by visiting Hitler in Berlin and openly sympathising with Nazism and its aspirations. George had managed to forestall his brother's attempts to return to Britain, thus converting what had begun as a temporary exile into the new beginnings of a permanent one. But it became increasingly clear that the Duke would demand a 'useful' and 'appropriate' wartime job, and that it would be as hard to deny him as it would to find a position in which he could do the least possible harm.

Right: *In Paris on a triumphant State Visit in July 1938, Queen Elizabeth's clothes were immensely admired.* Left: *A study in elegance by Cecil Beaton, this photograph was taken in the garden of Buckingham Palace the following year.*

*The State Opening of
Parliament, 8 November 1938.*

*A contrast three days later: Queen Elizabeth on Armistice Day on the balcony of the Home
Office with the Duchess of Kent, Princess Beatrice and Queen Mary.*

By contrast, the King and Queen were soon able to show how royal popularity can be turned to political advantage during a spectacular tour of the United States that summer, when their joint personal success in Roosevelt's Washington laid up a store of goodwill towards Britain that would prove invaluable in the years ahead. Apart from making a firm dent in the arguments of American isolationists, they were able to reassure doubters that it was not her nationality which the British establishment had held against the Duchess of Windsor. This first encounter with Franklin and Eleanor Roosevelt was to blossom into a genuine and much valued mutual friendship. As George and Elizabeth returned in triumph to Britain, having braved the apparent dangers of German submarines in the Atlantic, it was in their properly royal role of national symbols, representing Britannia's refusal to be daunted by the Nazi menace. It was the prelude to a time of great trial for Crown and people alike; but it was also the climax of a period of healing and reparation during which, as Edward VIII's biographer, Frances Donaldson, aptly put it,

The King and Queen's spectacular tour of the United States and Canada in the summer of 1939 was to pay dividends when Britain needed the goodwill of the two countries in the war. The King and Queen on the porch of Hyde Park, the Roosevelt home on the Hudson River, chat with the President, his wife Eleanor and mother Sarah.

King George VI and Queen Elizabeth had restored the stability of the Crown 'not by what they did but by what they were'.

It was King Edward VIII himself who had said that if the people wanted someone exactly like their father, then they should turn to the Duke of York. At moments like this King George VI did indeed share the endearing amazement expressed by his father, during his Silver Jubilee parade through London, that 'they really seem to like me – for myself'. Perhaps because of her own royal birth, Queen Mary was really too remote and formidable a figure to inspire the great public affection enjoyed by most royal females today; and the King himself was never the warmest or most charming of men. But George V nevertheless came to be respected by Britons for his evident integrity, his decency, his sense of honour and above all his conspicuous dedication to public service at whatever personal cost. These qualities had made him an inspirational wartime monarch. For much the same reasons – plus the added and invaluable bonus of a 'People's Queen' – the same was to prove true of his second son.

WAR

'This has made us.'

Four simple words expressed the King and Queen's exhilaration at their reception home from the United States. In London the crowds were as deep as on Coronation Day. The diarist Harold Nicolson was there, with a group of MPs playing truant from the Commons, and cheering as lustily as any: 'We lost all dignity and yelled and yelled. The King wore a happy schoolboy grin. The Queen was superb . . . She is in truth one of the most amazing Queens since Cleopatra.' Even after the King and Queen's appearance on the balcony of Buckingham Palace the huge throng just would not disperse. The royal dinner was eaten to a serenade of 'The Lambeth Walk' and 'Under the Spreading Chestnut Tree'; after another wave George and Elizabeth retired for the night, but it was midnight before the crowd trickled reluctantly home from the Mall.

The newspaper coverage relayed from the States had proved to Britons just how lucky they were to have this decent, dignified man and his bright-eyed, smiling Queen as national figureheads to set against the rantings of Herr Hitler. Elizabeth was voted Woman of the Year by readers of a syndicated American newspaper column and was reported as having 'a perfect genius' for her job by the novelist John Buchan, who as Lord Tweedsmuir, Governor-General of Canada, had received the royal couple on their way home. But Elizabeth derived even more delight from Bertie's success than from her own; at Guildhall next day, as he delivered a report of their trip, she was thrilled to hear Winston Churchill, the master orator, hail George VI as 'a fine public speaker'. Again the enthusiasm of the crowds was overwhelming. America had indeed been the making of them.

There was much to catch up on: apart from the backlog of routine royal work, the King received regular briefings from the Prime Minister and Foreign Secretary and held consultations with the heads of the three services about their preparations for war. George's proposal that he undertake a personal mission to Hitler was exhaustively discussed but finally vetoed; he was, however, to prove instrumental in the government's efforts to prove to the German Chancellor that Britain was now in deadly earnest.

That last summer of peace still held a few further pleasures before the lights of Europe began to go out again. In late July, before a final break to Balmoral, the King and Queen took their daughters with them on a visit to the Royal Naval College at Dartmouth, where a knowing smile played on the face of their friend Lord Mountbatten as he assigned his young nephew, Prince Philip of Greece, to look after Princess Elizabeth for the day. There followed, at the end of the summer break, one of the happiest and most successful of what were still known as the Duke of York's Camps; the King was pleased to find that, at forty-four, he could outpace his young charges as they followed deer tracks through the Highland heather. And so, at the end of August, back to London – and war. Elizabeth quickly followed her husband: 'If things turn out badly', she said, 'I must be with the King.'

On Sunday 3 September 1939, King George VI managed to avoid any hesitation in his voice – let alone any stammering, which he knew would now have a disastrous effect on national morale – as he made a solemn broadcast to his people: 'We are called, with our allies, to meet the challenge of a principle which, if it were to prevail, would be fatal to any civilised order in the world ... the primitive doctrine that Might is Right ... It is unthinkable that we should refuse to meet the challenge.'

Another equally unwelcome challenge quickly presented itself in the shape of the King's troublesome predecessor, the Duke of Windsor. When he had paid a secret visit to Windsor just before the war, George noted in his diary that his brother looked very well and seemed quite untroubled by memories of the abdication. 'He has forgotten all about it.' Now, with the

This photograph records probably the first occasion on which the future Queen Elizabeth II and the Duke of Edinburgh were pictured together. It was taken when the Royal Family visited the Dartmouth Naval College on 22 July 1939. The thirteen-year-old Princess Elizabeth in beret is on the left with Prince Philip just visible through the rails on the far right.

outbreak of hostilities, he was back, demanding front-rank wartime responsibilities for himself and his wife.

Most monarchs, George VI observed drily to a meeting of his military advisers, wear the crown only when their predecessors have died. 'Mine', he added, 'is not only alive, but very much so.' The Duke had gone behind the King's back to seek a tour of the military commands accompanied by his wife, who was then to be found a position in charge of a south coast hospital. 'The King', said his War Minister, Leslie Hoare-Belisha, 'seemed very disturbed. He paced up and down the room in a distressed state, saying that the Duke had never had any discipline in his life . . . He thought that if the Duchess went to the commands, particularly in Scotland, she might get a hostile reception.' George VI was adamant that the Duke and Duchess of Windsor were *not* to be permitted to tour the commands, but there was still the problem of what they *could* be found to do. To universal relief, the soldier and gentleman in the former monarch came to the fore when his King asked him to serve in the Military Mission in Paris. He accepted at once, even though it would mean relinquishing the rank of Field-Marshal automatically accorded him when he had become King. So the Windsors, as George VI had fervently hoped, were soon out of his kingdom again.

But they were not out of harm's way. After the German invasion of France, to the British government's unease, the Windsors wandered first to Madrid and then to Lisbon, where they were in frequent contact with emissaries from Hitler and Ribbentrop. The Duke is said to have declared himself 'against Churchill and the war', to have called his brother a man of 'copious stupidity', and to have accepted the role of Petain-style pawn in the event of a successful German invasion of Britain.

Attempts to shift him out of the reach of enemy agents, even if it meant his repatriation to Britain, foundered on the Duke's refusal to budge until his wife was accorded the cherished HRH. Both King and Government remained steadfast in their refusals, so the Windsors caused mounting concern by languishing in Estoril for some months until finally persuaded to accept the distant and humble, if comfortable, post of Governor of the Bahamas for the duration of the war. Even here, he was to remain the centre of recurrent rumours about kidnap plots and restoration intrigues.

For all his newfound confidence, Bertie was still wary of his brother's proven pulling-power as an alternative monarch – and he still looked up to him as a brighter and more capable individual than himself. Throughout their upbringing, as one contemporary put it, it had been 'like comparing an ugly duckling with a cock pheasant'. Now at last he had outmanoeuvred him, as well as proving a thoroughly competent monarch in his own right. The next six years were utterly to vindicate George's growing belief in himself, inculcated primarily by his wife's belief in him.

Aware that high public visibility was the greatest contribution she could make, the Queen leapt straight into action. During the uncertain days of the so-called 'phoney war', she travelled the length and breadth of the country in the royal train, visiting Red Cross centres and Civil Defence installations, air raid shelters and improvised hospitals, clothing factories and munition works, military training camps and evacuated children. After her visits to factories, it was noted, production figures would invariably improve. Attentive the while to matters of the spirit, she lent some paintings from Royal Lodge for exhibitions at the National Gallery, where she was also a conspicuous supporter of the famous lunchtime recitals which continued throughout the war. 'I have never seen the Queen more closely resemble her mother, Lady Strathmore, than she did in those first days of the war,' said one friend. 'She was a tower of strength.' And a member of her staff: 'The Queen never showed that she was worried.'

Lord Woolton, the Food Minister, has left us a touching vignette of the Queen Consort's priorities at this time. Having instituted a meals-on-wheels service requiring 'fearless and devoted' volunteers to undertake the deliveries, he sought her permission to call them the Queen's Messengers. 'But why *my* title?' she asked him. 'What will I have done?'

Daringly, he thought, Woolton replied: 'But Your Majesty, don't you know what you mean to all of us in this country? It isn't only your high position that matters; it is the fact that the

The King and Queen with the Prime Minister, Winston Churchill, inspect bomb damage at Buckingham Palace, which was hit altogether nine times during the war.

The King and Queen's stoic attitude to the Blitz is indicated by her famous remark, 'Now I can look the East End in the face.'

vast majority of people think of you as a person who would speak the kindly word, and, if it fell within your power, would take the cup of hot soup to the needy person.'

'Oh, my lord,' replied the Queen, putting her hands to her face, 'do you think I mean that? It is what I have tried so very hard to be.' It was, as Woolton put it in his memoirs, 'a very moving insight into the mind of a great lady'.

Elizabeth moved her daughters out of town – at first to Birkhall, on the Balmoral estate, and then to Windsor, where they were to see out the war. But the King and Queen themselves resolutely stayed on in Buckingham Palace – an act of defiance to the German bombers that came to symbolise their place at the head of an embattled nation, sharing every aspect of its ordeal. When it was put to her that the princesses should be shipped to America for the duration, Elizabeth wouldn't think of it: 'The children will not go without me,' she said. 'I won't leave the King. And of course the King will never leave.'

George and Elizabeth's conduct throughout the war has left a series of images still vivid to so many today: the King's secret visits to his troops; the Queen's to bomb-victims and evacuees; the broadcasts and whistle-stop tours to boost national morale; but above all this refusal to leave London even after the Palace was bombed. There was no attempt in those early days to build them any special kind of royal air-raid shelter. Whenever the sirens sounded, their Majesties – at a suitably dignified pace – simply went downstairs to join their staff in the basement.

Meanwhile a firing range was improvised in the Palace garden, which soon echoed to the rat-tat-tat of the King's determined tommy-gun training. Elizabeth joined in with a will. A variety of gung-ho remarks have been attributed to her – 'They won't take me easily', for instance, and 'I shan't go down like the others' (meaning the several royal houses of Europe which had fallen in recent years); and Elizabeth alarmed not merely her staff by the enthusiasm with which she took to her daily target practice. Lord Halifax, the Foreign Secretary, had been granted the privilege of crossing the Palace garden as a short cut to Whitehall; on seeing the Queen and her ladies peppering shots all round the target one day, he discreetly changed his daily route.

Hearing of all this, and admiring the bulldog spirit it signified, Winston Churchill sent round a particularly lethal American revolver which became the Queen's favourite weapon. It was a gesture which would stand him in good stead when the events of the following summer pitched him into one of the closest alliances every enjoyed between a prime minister and his monarch.

On 9 April 1940, Germany invaded Denmark and Norway. Though in on the tactical discussions in the Admiralty War Room, the King was filled with memories of his brief taste of Naval action in the First War, and felt miserably impotent. 'A bad day,' he told his diary. 'Everybody working at fever heat except me.'

Not for long, however. The following month saw Tory rebels joining the Labour opposition in their famous cry 'In the name of God, go!', which ended the premiership of Neville Chamberlain. The King, whose emotional resistance to the thought of another war had led him to support Chamberlain and his policy of appeasement, was dismayed by his downfall. Now he found himself at the heart of a constitutional crisis. Rather than follow traditional procedures and invite the leader of the next largest party, Clement Attlee, to try to form a government (which, most historians agree, he would anyway not have been able to do), George suggested that Chamberlain, as Conservative leader, name his successor. At a round-table meeting in the Palace, he and the King were joined by Halifax and Churchill – who emerged as the embattled nation's new political leader. 'I have nothing to offer,' he memorably declared, 'but blood, toil, tears and sweat.'

George was again disappointed. He had favoured Halifax and it was to take some time before he could reconcile himself to Churchill, let alone warm to the man who had so vociferously supported his brother's cause during the abdication crisis. 'I cannot yet think of Winston as PM,' he wrote on 11 May. 'I met Halifax in the garden, and told him I was sorry not to have him as PM.' But by the end of the year he was able to say, 'I could not have a better Prime Minister'. The degree of intimacy which developed between them, said Churchill himself, was 'without precedent since the days of Queen Anne and Marlborough'.

It was Churchill's profound respect for the monarchy, George came to realise, which had led him to fight against an abdication in 1936. As they spent more time together, in ever more difficult days, it became clear that they had a great deal in common: a high degree of intelligence and integrity, to be sure, but above all an aggressive patriotism which would brook no thought of defeat or surrender. Over their weekly sandwich lunches, at which Elizabeth often acted as waitress, they forged a bond of mutual respect which was to be of the utmost importance to the nation's morale. One day George and Churchill gave the Queen a quizzical glance as they tucked into the austerity rations she had served. 'I don't know what on earth is in these sandwiches', said King to Prime Minister. 'Sawdust, I suppose.'

As more neighbour nations fell to Hitler's advance, the Palace became a royal refugee centre for the ousted crowned heads of Europe. When King Haakon of Norway joined Queen Wilhelmina of the Netherlands under Elizabeth's roof in 1940,

The King and Queen chatting to workmen after an air raid had damaged buildings in West London.

both were appalled by the lack of security around the British royals, convinced as they were that Hitler aimed to kidnap monarchs and hold them as symbols of their nations' subjugation.

'What would happen', asked Wilhelmina, 'if German paratroopers started landing in that garden right now?' Smiling confidently, King George VI pressed a special alarm button and invited his guests to join him at the window to watch the resulting rush to action stations. They watched and watched . . . but nothing happened. In response to the King's angry inquiries, the duty guard reported that he had checked with the police, who reported no warnings of any raid, and so decided it must have been a false alarm. Security was immediately stepped up; the King and Queen rode in a bullet-proof car; there were elaborate plans for action in the event of a kidnap attempt – and the King at last agreed to have a proper air-raid shelter built within the Palace precincts.

In September 1940 the Blitz began in earnest, to find George and Elizabeth again conspicuously sharing the sufferings of their subjects. One early air raid caught them on a tour of East London Civil Defence centres, so that they joined East Enders

The King and Queen sheltering in the London underground after an alert sounded as they were making a tour.

106

in a public shelter, sharing their cups of tea. One of the first buildings to be completely razed was their former home, 145 Piccadilly (the Inter-Continental Hotel now stands where once it looked out on Hyde Park Corner). Which also gave them something in common with a great many of their people. Throughout that month George and Elizabeth were almost daily to be found at the site of the previous night's raids, offering comfort and sympathy to those deprived of their homes, even their loved ones. 'For him we had admiration, for her adoration,' said the recipient of one such visit. 'Many an aching heart', wrote Churchill, 'found solace in her gracious smile.'

Vivid though these scenes were all over the capital, it was somehow in the East End that they were at their most potent. One of the most famous remarks of that awful year came from a Cockney woman who watched as the Queen helped a mother with a disabled arm to dress her baby. 'Oh, ain't she lovely,' came the Cockney cry. 'Ain't she just *bloody* lovely.'

On 13 September the Palace was bombed again. This time the King and Queen only narrowly escaped serious injury, if not death. 'We were both upstairs in my little sitting-room,' George recalled. 'All of a sudden we heard an aircraft making a zooming noise above us, saw 2 bombs falling past the opposite side of the Palace, & then heard 2 resounding crashes as the bombs fell in the quadrangle about thirty yards away. We looked at each other, & then we were out into the passage as fast as we could get there. The whole thing happened in a matter of seconds. We all wondered why we weren't dead.'

They were lucky not to be. As Churchill wrote in his history of the Second World War, even he as Prime Minister did not realise until some years later how close to death they had been: 'I must confess that at the time neither I nor any of my colleagues were aware of the peril of this particular incident. Had the windows been closed instead of open, the whole of the glass would have splintered into the faces of the King and Queen, causing terrible injuries. So little did they make of it that even I, who saw them and their entourage so frequently, only realised long afterwards what had actually happened.'

Top: *On a visit to Birmingham the King and Queen watch the production of two-pounder tracer shells*. Above: *Talking to tin miners in Cornwall about their work. Throughout the war the King and Queen shared the dangers with the people, travelling half a million miles up and down the country in the royal train.*

Six bombs had been dropped with impressive accuracy. There were two large craters in the Palace forecourt; all the windows looking on to that courtyard were smashed; and the Chapel was completely wrecked (never, as it transpired, to be rebuilt; today the Queen's Picture Gallery, the only part of the Palace open to the Public, stands where once the chapel was). The King and Queen went down to the basement to check on their staff: all well, except for four men wounded in the plumber's workshop. In light-hearted manner, the Queen made a soon-to-be-famous remark to a sheltering policeman: 'I'm almost glad we've been bombed. Now I can look the East End in the face.'

It is a phrase which will reverberate through the history of the British monarchy's relations with its people. Never before, or indeed since, had such a strength of fellow-feeling been so genuine and so widely shared. As Churchill wrote to them, when the Palace had been bombed for the ninth time: 'This war has drawn the throne and the people more closely together than ever before, and Your Majesties are more beloved by all classes and conditions of people than any princes of the past.' The Home Secretary, Herbert Morrison, avowed that the King and Queen did more than anyone or anything else to keep the nation's spirits up. An American admirer sent the Queen a verse tribute.

> *Be it said to your renown*
> *That you wore your gayest gown,*
> *Your bravest smile, and stayed in Town*
> *When London Bridge was burning down,*
> *My Fair Lady . . .*

Years later, when Elizabeth received the Freedom of the City of London, the citation read: 'During the full weight of the enemy attack on London, the Queen became the shining symbol of her sex. Wherever the bombs fell thickest, there she was to be found bringing comfort and encouragement to the homeless.' As the German bombing missions spread further afield, the same was true in many other British cities such as Coventry and Cardiff, Plymouth and Liverpool, Manchester and Bath, Bristol and Birmingham. The King was with her whenever his duties would permit. As the war ground on they travelled more than half a million miles all over the country in the royal train, from which George kept in touch with developments by a special telephone link to Churchill.

Elizabeth meanwhile turned the Palace into an engine-room of the war effort, its ornate, gilt-edged chambers becoming the headquarters for her many working parties, mass-producing surgical dressings and 'comforters' for British troops. Eleanor Roosevelt, a visitor in 1942, testified that conditions were no more comfortable in the Palace than elsewhere around the land. The Queen had given her distinguished guest her own bedroom, which had wooden boards instead of windows and was heated by a one-bar electric radiator. The food was very sparse, Mrs Roosevelt wrote to her husband, and 'the Palace is enormous, and without heat. Both the King and Queen have colds.'

By then, of course, America had been drawn into the conflict, following the Japanese attack on Pearl Harbor in December 1941. Up to that point, King and President had corresponded frequently and candidly. Churchill was in no doubt that the friendship which grew from that 1939 visit had been of great assistance not just in combating isolationism but in winning the much-needed ships, weapons and other Lend-Lease supplies which had compromised American neutrality in the early stages of the war. Mrs Roosevelt's mission was to visit, as her husband's representative, the American troops who were arriving in Britain in ever increasing numbers. The letter she carried from her husband to the King gives a clear measure of the intimacy which had developed between them: 'I want you and the Queen to tell Eleanor everything in regard to problems of our troops in England which she might not get from Government or military authorities. You and I know that it is the little things which count but which are not always set forth in the official reports.'

It was during a Palace dinner party in Mrs Roosevelt's honour, in November 1942, that Churchill left the room to telephone Downing Street and returned singing 'Roll Out the Barrel'. He was then able to announce the news of Montgomery's victory at El Alamein. The tide was beginning to turn. George VI wrote to his Prime Minister: 'When I look back & think of all the many arduous hours of work you have put in & the many miles you have travelled to bring this battle to a successful conclusion, you have every right to rejoice; while the rest of our people will one day be very thankful to you for what you have done. I cannot say more.'

The King had been deeply affected by the death of his youngest brother George, the Duke of Kent, when flying a mission in appalling weather conditions over Scotland the previous August. This was the man who might have been King in his stead, and although only a handful of people knew this at the time, the Duke was a conspicuous and popular figure whose death stunned the nation. The war itself had also brought the royal brothers much closer together. Now, as if to take on the Duke of Kent's work as well, the King decided the time was right for him to take a few of the risks his advisers had been urging against, and venture abroad on the first of a series of visits to his troops in the field. For Elizabeth they were nervous times – doubly so because her husband's absence had to be kept utterly secret until he was safely returned. As she wrote to Queen Mary in June 1943:

> I have had a few anxious hours because at 8.15 I heard that the plane had been heard near Gibraltar and that it would soon be landing. Then after an hour and a half I heard that there was thick fog at Gib., and that they were going on to Africa. Then complete silence till a few minutes ago, when a message came that they had landed in Africa and taken off again. Of course, I imagined every sort of horror, and walked up and down in my room staring at the telephone ...

Elizabeth had her own anxious moment one evening at Windsor, where she was dressing for dinner when she suddenly felt a hand gripping her ankle. It turned out to belong to an intruder who had hidden himself earlier that day behind her bedroom curtains – a deserter who had bluffed his way into the royal apartments in the hope of winning the Queen's sympathy. After summoning assistance and then giving him a fairer hearing than perhaps he deserved, she concluded that there was nothing to justify special treatment: the man was a 'malingerer', whose plight was no worse than that of the hundreds of suffering people she saw every day. His self-pity brought out the stern patriot in the Queen. 'I advise you to take your punishment like a man,' she told him as he was led away, 'and to serve your country like one.' (She made so light of what could have been a much uglier incident that few recalled it when her daughter, the Queen, was herself surprised by an intruder in her bedroom at Buckingham Palace in 1982.)

By spring 1944, King and Prime Minister were able to join in the planning of D-Day, the landings in Europe codenamed Operation Overlord. Both, unknown to the other, were making private plans to be there. George had already secured Elizabeth's reluctant agreement by the end of May, when Churchill told the King he planned to watch the first attack from the bridge of one of the forward ships; George, who had known nothing of this, told an equally astonished Churchill: 'So do I.' A horrified Sir Alan Lascelles, the King's private secretary, somewhat sarcastically asked the King and Queen whether they had ensured that their elder daughter was familiar with both the rites of succession and the procedures for choosing a new Prime Minister, in the event that both men were to be killed. George took the point and reluctantly abandoned the idea, only to be dismayed by Churchill's refusal to follow suit. He wrote his PM a tetchy, slightly jealous note:

I am a younger man than you, I am a sailor, & as King I am the head of all three services. There is nothing I would like better than to go to sea but I have agreed to stop at home. Is it fair that you should then do exactly what I would have liked to do myself? You said yesterday afternoon that it would be a fine thing for the King to lead his troops into battle, as in old days; if the King cannot do this, it does not seem to me right that his Prime Minister should take his place...

When Churchill failed to answer the note and left Downing Street for General Eisenhower's headquarters at Portsmouth, the King made ready to drive down personally at dawn next day to prevent him sailing with the Fleet. Luckily, however, Lascelles managed first to get hold of the Prime Minister on the telephone, and at last to persuade him to call off his bravura performance.

Despite all this, George managed to cross to France by night on 15 June, just over a week after D-Day, and watch the progress of the invasion for himself. 'I got a very good view', he reported, 'of the mass of shipping which is there stretching for miles in both directions . . . The cruiser *Hawkins* was actually firing in support of an attack as we came in.' He landed by amphibious craft, to be met by Montgomery and briefed on the course of the battle. 'The position at Caen', the King concluded, 'is the most delicate.'

This was also the week that the Germans unleashed on London their most devastating weapon yet, the V1 flying bombs. These pilotless, high-explosive planes were feared above all else for the chilling few seconds of silence between the cut-out of the engine and the massive explosion which ensued. As the Queen said: 'There is something very inhuman about death-dealing missiles being launched in such an indiscriminate manner.' The Palace was again a target, all its windows and much of its surrounding wall being destroyed. The V1s were soon replaced by the even deadlier V2s, rockets which fell from the sky without any sonic warning, causing hundreds of deaths and thousands of serious injuries. The end of the war in Europe was in sight; but the people of London were still suffering the grimmest and most testing of winters.

It was a bitter personal loss for both George and Elizabeth when the newly re-elected President Roosevelt, having just accepted their invitation to visit London that summer, died suddenly and unexpectedly during a Georgia vacation in April 1945. The King ordered a week of court mourning and led mourners at a memorial service at St Paul's. It was a grim, unspoken reminder of the toll the war had taken on George's own health; since 1942 he had reluctantly put on tan make-up before public appearances, in an attempt to hide his unflagging efforts. But now the home straight was in sight; in early May, Churchill telephoned Sandringham with confirmation that it was now only a matter of days.

On 8 May 1945 the Prime Minister joined the King and Queen on the balcony of a newly floodlit Buckingham Palace to take no fewer than eight VE-Day 'curtain calls'. All looked deathly tired; but the exhilaration of the moment gave them renewed stamina as half a million people cried 'We want the King!' 'We want the Queen!' The two princesses, had earlier been out in the crowd, enjoying the victory ritual of knocking people's hats off; now they too – Elizabeth in uniform – joined the triumphant group on the Palace balcony. It was a victory celebration the like of which this country had never seen before.

Princess Elizabeth's eighteenth birthday, 21 April 1944. Back row: *the Duke and Duchess of Gloucester, Princess Margaret and the Earl of Harewood.* Front row: *Queen Mary, King George VI, Princess Elizabeth and Queen Elizabeth.*

The Royal family on the balcony of Buckingham Palace during the VE Day celebrations, 8 May 1945 – the exhilaration of the moment gave them all renewed energy.

3
Queen Mother

WIDOW

Now that it was at last all over, the King described himself as 'burnt out'. The whole family, he told his new Prime Minister, Clement Attlee, was 'down to the lowest ebb'. The Queen described herself, in a letter to Queen Mary, as 'quite exhausted after seeing so much sadness, sorrow, heroism and magnificent spirit. The destruction is so awful and the people are so wonderful – they deserve a better world.'

When they opened parliament together for the new session – the King far from happy about the post-war change of government – Elizabeth was accorded three cheers in her own right as she and her husband processed down the aisle separating Lords from Commons. Harold Nicolson described her regal progress in terms often repeated since: 'The Queen has a truly miraculous faculty of making each individual feel that it is him who she has greeted, and to him that was devoted that lovely smile. She has a true genius for her job.'

King and Queen had less than seven years left together, but it was to prove a much happier period than those pre-war years on the throne. Thanks primarily to the rigours of war, both now regarded the monarchy as a duty to which they had grown seasoned, more than a burden they would rather have avoided. The King had grown hugely in self-confidence and international stature: his nerves before his annual radio broadcasts (live in those days) may have ruined his Christmas lunch, but there was no more stammering. It was, he would tell friends, all due to his wife.

'*She* helps me,' he said simply to Lady Airlie, when she asked the King how he was coping. Now nearly eighty, the confidante of both Elizabeth and Bertie since their youth was still on hand

The King taking the salute during London's victory procession, 8 July 1946.

to record the post-war change of mood, and to note the strains upon the King. At Sandringham, for instance, 'no medals or orders were worn at dinner time; it was much more like ordinary family life than it had been in the old days. It was in the way in which the King said "You must ask Mummy" when his daughters wanted to do something . . . in Princess Margaret's pout when the Queen sent her back to the house to put on a thicker coat . . . in the way both sisters teased, and were teased by, the young Guardsmen.'

At dinner that night Lady Airlie sat next to George VI. 'His face was tired and strained and he ate practically nothing. I knew that he was forcing himself to talk and to entertain me. He had worked on his Boxes right up to dinner time and afterwards went back to them again. It was obvious how hard he was driving himself.'

The change of government, to George, was just another burden. He missed his chatty lunches with his friend Churchill, and found the new Cabinet members 'rather difficult to talk to'.

He was distressed when one of them, Aneurin Bevan, refused to wear evening dress, describing it as 'upper-class uniform', and found only the new Foreign Secretary, Ernest Bevin, 'good . . . he tells me everything that is going on'. The rest were 'still learning how to run their departments, and their efforts have not made life any easier so far'.

Because of his unusually intimate involvement with government during the war, George VI was now rather closer to the political process than a modern constitutional monarch expects to be. As Dickie Mountbatten had written to him at the war's end: 'You will find that your position will be greatly strengthened, since you are now the old experienced campaigner on whom a new and partly inexperienced Government will lean for advice and guidance.' And this at a time when America too had a new leader, President Harry Truman – and when the decisions being made were as momentous as that to drop the first atomic bombs on Japan.

Elizabeth encouraged her husband to escape from the strain of it all by guiding him back to his more domestic pursuits. Gardening, for instance, always an absorbing interest, now became a passion; the grounds around all the royal homes underwent extensive redesign and replanting. Fishing too could now return to the daily agenda at Balmoral, where both King and Queen were delighted to find their elder daughter, Lilibet, joining them with equal enthusiasm and skill.

Princess Margaret, by contrast, was developing a character almost wilfully in contrast to that of her elder sister. To the family she was 'a holy terror', swigging defiantly from the sherry bottle and using slang jargon she said she had picked up 'at my mother's knee, or some such low joint'. Always a more extrovert, dynamic personality than her elder sister, she was less concerned than Lilibet to share her father's enjoyment of traditional family pursuits, such as shooting. Queen Mary rather liked this apparent reincarnation of the young Victoria, finding Margaret 'so outrageously amusing that one can't help encouraging her'. But her own immediate family – as with Edward, Prince of Wales, a decade and more before – were perhaps not quite as alert as they might have been to the

One of the happiest episodes of Queen Elizabeth's life was the family's tour of South Africa in 1947. The Queen holds a model zebra while Princess Elizabeth looks on. Standing on the Queen's right are Princess Margaret and Group Captain Peter Townsend, soon to play a significant role in the life of the Queen's younger daughter.

auguries in Margaret's behaviour of the storm to come so early in her sister's reign. She was only fourteen, but her hero-worship of one of her father's equerries, Group Captain Peter Townsend, had already taken root.

For Margaret's parents the years 1946–47 were dominated by two very different concerns, one public and one private, the first being the end of British rule in India. It was Attlee who suggested Dickie Mountbatten to preside over the dissolution of Empire, and the King who talked his reluctant cousin into it. Once the royal family had realised the political necessities and overcome their natural reluctance to shed yet more of their national heritage, the most poignant effect of Indian independence upon them was that King George VI perforce dropped the word 'Imperator' from his official title. One of the Queen Mother's many unique distinctions, therefore, is that she will go down in history as the last British Empress.

Princess Elizabeth, meanwhile, as far as her parents could tell, appeared to have fallen in love with the first eligible bachelor she had met. After that initial pre-war meeting at

121

Princess Elizabeth lent the Queen her shoes after she had damaged her own while climbing the Matopos Hills in Bulawayo.

Dartmouth, under the matchmaking auspices of Mountbatten, she and Prince Philip of Greece and Denmark had kept in constant touch. At the end of the war she told her parents she was in love with him, that she had been for several years, and now wished to marry him. She was still only nineteen.

George and Elizabeth counselled caution. Quite apart from the familiar anxieties of traditionally-minded parents about so headstrong a romance, there were political problems: civil strife in Greece; and British disaffection with Philip's native Germany. As he and Elizabeth reluctantly agreed to her parents' insistence on delay, at least until her twenty-first birthday, Philip was persuaded quietly to shed his awkward birthright and become plain Lieutenant Philip Mountbatten RN.

It was during this 'cooling-off period', in 1947, that George and Elizabeth enjoyed one of the happiest episodes of both their lives, as the entire family set off together to tour South Africa. It was a triumphant progress, in balmy weather, which did

One of the highlights of the King and Queen's last years together was the birth of their first grandchild, Prince Charles, in November 1948. The Prince is wearing the royal Christening robe of white silk and Honiton lace made for Queen Victoria's children.

The King and Queen attending the Silver Wedding thanksgiving service in St. Paul's Cathedral . . .

much to charge the weary royal batteries. Marked by Princess Elizabeth's moving twenty-first birthday broadcast, in which she dedicated her life to the service of Britain and the Commonwealth, the tour is also remembered for one of her mother's most characteristic one-liners. When one of their Boer hosts declared he would never be able to forgive the British for annexing his country, she promptly replied: 'I know. We feel very much the same in Scotland.'

Those few remaining years together were to hold many more highlights, chief among them their elder daughter's wedding to Philip in November 1947, followed by the births of their first grandchildren. November 1948 saw the arrival of the infant Prince Charles to ensure the succession, and their own silver wedding anniversary, a moment for celebration and re-dedication. After a thanksgiving service at St Paul's and a splendid procession through London, the crowds which drew them again and again on to the Palace balcony reaffirmed how much this couple now meant to their people. In the words of the Archbishop of Canterbury: 'The Nation and the Empire bless God that He has set such a family at the seat of our Royalty.'

But the King was already suffering from the leg pains that were the beginning of the end. For a while in 1948, the onset of arteriosclerosis led to a danger of gangrene. The Queen spent mid-November smiling her way to and from two improvised hospital suites in Buckingham Palace, in one of

. . . and in their carriage on the return journey to Buckingham Palace, 26 April 1948.

The King and Queen, followed by Princess Margaret, leave the Drury Lane Theatre after seeing the show South Pacific *on 30 January 1952. Within a week the King was dead . . .*

The only time in history when Britain had three Queens at the same time. At the funeral of King George VI his mother, Queen Mary, his wife Queen Elizabeth and the present Queen, then the Princess Elizabeth, await the arrival of the coffin for the Lying-in-State.

which her daughter was preparing to give birth, while in the other her husband faced the possibility of the amputation of his right leg. Elizabeth had to prevent either worrying about the other, and so took the anxieties of both upon herself. Over the next three years several royal tours had to be called off because of the King's failing health, aggravated by Britain's growing domestic problems and then the Korean War. At the end of 1951, George summed up a dismal year in his diary: 'The incessant worries and crises through which we have to live got me down something proper.'

He did not, alas, have to live through them much longer. King George VI died in his sleep at Sandringham on 6 February 1952. He was only fifty-six years old, his widow just fifty-one. 'My only wish now', she said in a message to the nation, 'is that I may be allowed to continue the work that we sought to do together.'

Elizabeth took it very hard. She might so easily, like Queen Victoria after the death of *her* Bertie, have succumbed to her private grief and retreated from public life. That certainly was her mood that winter, when her 25-year-old daughter was propelled on to the throne earlier than she too would have wished, for the sake not just of her father but of her children.

The widowed Queen's first concern, characteristically, was more for her daughter than herself. When many of the Buckingham Palace staff declared it their wish to move with her to Clarence House, she regretfully persuaded most that it was their duty to serve their new monarch – who was in the greater need of their support. And just five days into the new reign, with a calm efficiency which would have pleased her husband, she formally announced that she wished henceforth to be known as Queen Elizabeth the Queen Mother. It is not a title the Royal Family particularly likes, nor one which had been used in the recent past; but it was necessary to find a formula which avoided confusion between the two Elizabeths, the new Queen and the old. Even today, in royal circles, the title 'the Queen Mother' is rarely used. The Queen Dowager (a title she dislikes even more) is referred to as Queen Elizabeth, her daughter simply as The Queen.

In 1952 the new Queen Mother lent every support she could to the young new Queen privately, while keeping publicly out of her way. For some months she went north to nurse her bereavement at Birkhall, the home on the Balmoral estate she had shared with Bertie in the early years of their marriage, and to which she now returned from the Castle. Here she sadly declined the suggestions of her anxious staff that she entertain friends. 'Oh no,' she would say, 'they won't want to come . . . No one really understands.'

She wore black for a year. On the rare occasions she was persuaded to venture out, even make a speech, she would not risk her composure by mentioning her husband's name. When old Princess Marie Louise told her what a brave face she was putting on things, she replied quietly: 'Not in private.'

One day at Birkhall that first summer, the Queen Mother received a visit from her loyal friend Winston Churchill, by now reinstalled where she and Bertie had always thought he belonged, in Downing Street. No one knows to this day what passed between Prime Minister and Queen Dowager, but somehow the crafty old magician talked her round. It is from this moment that the Royal Family dates Queen Elizabeth's determination to re-emerge into society – and thus the beginnings of the long and remarkable Indian summer of her life, to so many its crowning glory.

If there is no role written into the British constitution for a Queen Consort, still less is one prescribed for a Queen Dowager – or Queen Mother. What she makes of it is really up to her. This one chose to plunge herself back into public service with a conviction and stamina which are the envy of her family and the pride of the nation. It is no exaggeration to say that she has singlehandedly invented a whole new type of royal persona. As Britain and the Commonwealth celebrate her eighty-fifth birthday, the former Lady Elizabeth Bowes-Lyon seems to have lived several lives, all with great vigour and success.

Born into the Scottish gentry, she reluctantly became a royal duchess, then even more reluctantly a Queen. And now she is well into her fourth decade as a widow, a Queen Mother who has carved for herself a brand new niche in the royal escutcheon. She may not like the title, but the second half of her life has certainly seen her become the most popular Queen Dowager in the history of these islands. The two other

CHAPTER SEVEN

Dowagers of recent memory, Queen Alexandra and Queen Mary, were almost entirely private people after their husbands' deaths, the subject of rumour, gossip and malicious jokes as they grew sterner, more distant, more formidable figures. Queen Elizabeth, by contrast, has plunged back into public life with renewed dedication and a vigour remarkably undimmed by the years.

The widowed Queen's first major public reappearance came nearly eighteen months after the King's death, at their daughter's coronation in June 1953. As George VI's had been the first coronation to be broadcast by radio, so Elizabeth II's was the first to be televised. A delighted nation was able to watch as the Queen Mother looked after four-year-old Prince Charles during the service, gently pulling him back as he leant dangerously far over the gallery rail. The young heir apparent was also observed to wipe some of the grease from his slicked-back hair and transfer it to his grandmother's hand, apparently in the hope that she would enjoy the smell. It was, despite the rain, a triumphant day, and the Queen Mother received another special cheer when the balcony group parted that evening to allow her a grand entry.

It had been a day largely for maternal pride in the capable, very solemn way in which her young daughter took up the 'intolerable burden' she had inherited. But to Queen Elizabeth such moments held memories of her late husband too poignant to be undergone too often. Always modest enough to assume that it was his memory people were cheering rather than her presence, she decided to soft-pedal public appearances in Britain, preferring to let her daughter establish her own public persona as Queen – and instead embarked with some relish on a long series of overseas journeys. This, besides, was a time for youth. Stage-managed by that great romantic Winston Churchill, who after initial anxieties had developed a soft spot for his new young Queen, Britons on all sides were heralding the dawn of a new Elizabethan era, marked by the glitter and energy of youth. The Queen Mother felt she should stay in the shadows. If she were to carry on the work she had begun with her husband, she would do so, for now, abroad.

128

The Queen Mother's first major public reappearance after the King's death came at the coronation of their daughter in Westminster Abbey, 2 June 1953.

Only that May this genteel lady, born before the age of the motor car, had had the national heart in its mouth when she decided to sample the jet age. Following the inaugural flight of the Comet, the world's first passenger jet, she had asked for a spin – and was duly taken up, along with Princess Margaret, by BOAC's chief test pilot, John Cunningham. The then BOAC chairman, Miles Thomas, described in his memoirs what happened when the Queen Mother swapped her high-heels for some casuals and took the controls somewhere over the Alps:

Her Majesty eased the control forward, the Comet gathered speed. Cunningham gave her a little extra throttle, the Mach needle crept towards the coloured danger sector and suddenly the Comet began to porpoise. Not violently, but just enough to indicate that we had reached the limits of her stability. Quickly John eased the throttles back, Her Majesty did the same with the controls, and we went back to the same cruising speed as before the royal sprint . . .

129

The flight, as Thomas points out, was of course before the series of crashes the Comet subsequently suffered through structural weakness. 'Had that porpoising gone on much longer, the wracking on the structure could well have precipitated a rupture of the skin of the kind that caused the subsequent tragedies. I still shudder every time I think of that flight.' It was the first of several such false alarms, which reached their climax thirty years later when the obstinacy of a Windsor fishbone had the octogenarian Queen Mother on an operating table and the nation anxiously holding its breath.

It was nevertheless by Comet that she flew the following month (again with Princess Margaret) on her first overseas tour as Queen Mother, to open the Rhodes Centenary Exhibition in Bulawayo, Southern Rhodesia. The trip was naturally filled with memories of her first official trip abroad with her husband, and was to be the first of many she made to Africa after his death. It is a continent to which throughout her life Queen Elizabeth has responded in a particularly warm and emotional way (as does Prince Charles, for instance, to Australasia).

'Who is going to be interested in the middle-aged widow of a King?' was her reaction on being invited back to the United States – this time to take formal receipt of the money raised for a fund in King George VI's memory, which would enable young people from the Commonwealth to undergo technical training in America. Plenty of people, was the answer of the *New York Times*: 'Of all the many reasons for welcoming Queen Elizabeth the Queen Mother, the pleasantest is that she is so nice . . .'

She went reluctantly, and regarded the visit as something of an experiment. Were people abroad, even Americans, *really* interested in her in her own right? To return to the scene of their memorable 1939 visit to the Roosevelts, this time alone, would be a stern test indeed. She sailed out on her eponymous liner, the *Queen Elizabeth*, where she found herself applauded by her fellow-passengers every time she set foot outside her private quarters. And, of course, she took New York by storm; huge crowds cheered her arrival at the Empire State Building and later followed her into Saks Fifth Avenue. At the heart of her visit, after the ceremony for the King George VI Fund had been televised live coast-to-coast, one New York newspaper summed up: 'The royal lady with the peaches-and-cream complexion and twinkling eyes not only drew a record crowd of 2,800 smart-setters to the Waldorf Astoria ballroom; she sent them away humming "God save the Queen" like a first-night audience whistling the top tunes of a hit show.' Another newspaper spoke of 'the royal lady with the peaches-and-cream complexion and the twinkling orbs'. Between them New Yorkers, during that visit, gave Elizabeth the one nickname which has stuck: 'The Queen Mum'. Her international reputation assured, Queen Elizabeth returned home to find her daughter at the centre of her first real crisis as monarch – and it centred around her own Household, in the shape of its Comptroller, Group Captain Peter Townsend.

Townsend had been George VI's personal choice as one of his Equerries of Honour, in recognition of his 'outstanding leadership, organisation and determination' during the war. He had quickly won a special place in the King's favour, so much so that he and his wife were given a grace-and-favour residence near Windsor, and the King was pleased to become godfather to their second child. He had played a large part in the organisation of the 1947 tour of South Africa and had accompanied the royal party, with the particular role of looking after the young princesses while their parents were busy with official duties.

Princess Elizabeth was then, of course, pining for her Philip, so it is not surprising that rather more of Townsend's time was spent with Margaret. Similar ironies piled up in the ensuing years. As King George VI grew more ill, it was to his trusted aide Townsend that Queen Elizabeth turned for male advice and company. And it was the demands of his job – working late at the Palace and being regularly summoned back from home after hours, both before and after the King's death – which led to the failure of Townsend's marriage; in late 1953 he obtained a divorce on the grounds of his wife's adultery.

After the King's death, when the new Queen was suddenly

immersed in affairs of state, her sister felt not merely left out of things but rather lonely. Again, the man she turned to for solace was the man closest to her family's daily life at Clarence House: Townsend, chosen by her mother to take charge of the running of her day-to-day life. Their enforced friendship grew into a very genuine love between a young princess and a somewhat older courtier. Their wish to marry was a worrying secret to the Queen throughout her coronation year, during which her prime minister, Churchill, advised that a marriage between the Queen's sister and a divorced commoner would not be acceptable.

The public knew nothing of all this until 2 June 1953, the day of Elizabeth II's coronation. At the end of the ceremony, as official guests waited for their carriages, the new Queen's sister was seen to pick some threads of fluff off Townsend's uniform – an overtly affectionate gesture which gave the press the excuse it had been waiting for. For a few days, as in 1936, British newspapers dithered over the sensational story bandied about by their continental brethren; but that weekend, with the bleak hypocrisy characteristic of Britain's 'popular' Sunday newspapers, the *Sunday People* decided that the only way to print the rumours was to deny them. In its most sanctimonious tone of voice, the *People* callously declared that it was of course 'quite unthinkable that a royal princess, third in line of succession to the throne, should even contemplate a marriage with a man who has been through the divorce courts'.

Thus began the ordeal of Princess Margaret which remains so acutely poignant today, after the marriage she was to contract instead has also failed. It was as a royal princess 'mindful of the Church's teaching that a Christian marriage is indissoluble', that Margaret finally denied herself potential happiness with Townsend, who discreetly disappeared from the scene. Five years later, in 1960, she married the photographer Antony Armstrong-Jones, later ennobled as Lord Snowdon. Constitutional niceties take little note of social change, but the speed with which social mores have relaxed in the second half of the twentieth century has at last been reflected by those of the Royal Family. It is just such a sign of

The funeral service for the Duke of Windsor took place at St George's Chapel, Windsor, on 5 June 1972. The Queen Mother follows the Duchess of Windsor and Queen Elizabeth out of the Chapel – two Queens and the lady who might have been.

the royal times that, twenty-five years after refusing her sister permission to marry a divorcée, Elizabeth II let her divorce the man she had married instead.

It was in the midst of the Townsend affair that Queen Elizabeth unveiled a memorial in the Mall to her much-missed husband, King George VI, reminding onlookers that 'He shirked no task, however difficult, and to the end he never faltered in his duty.' That some commentators have taken these remarks as a coded message to Princess Margaret, reminding her where her duty lay, is really an index of how strikingly little the Queen Mother intervened in her daughter's dilemma. As with the abdication crisis in 1936, she seemed merely to crumple slightly under the worry of it all, and watch anxiously from a distance.

133

Others, to be sure, had more central constitutional roles; but few had so strong a right to express a personal opinion as Princess Margaret's and mother. Like her elder daughter the Queen, Queen Elizabeth has never revealed her personal views on the rights and wrongs of the Townsend affair. However, it does seem likely that so fond and strong-minded a mother would have argued her daughter's case more forcefully if the marriage had in fact privately had her blessing. The same was to prove true of Margaret's separation and divorce from Lord Snowdon in 1976–78. The Queen Mother confided to friends her personal grief at Margaret's unhappiness, but left the real decisions to her elder daughter – her own unique way of blending formal disapproval with private sympathy. In the minds of her daughter's subjects, however, Queen Elizabeth the Queen Mother somehow rises effortlessly above these rare royal controversies. She is seen simply as a fond maternal figure lurking in the background, buffeted by the unfair effects of the British constitution on her otherwise unshakeable faith in traditional family values.

It was the Queen Mother who took in Lady Diana Spencer, in the early weeks of her engagement to the Prince of Wales, for what amounted to a 'crash course' in the art of being royal. She may have tut-tutted slightly at breakfast, the morning after Di's first big night out in that famous low-cut black dress; but 'Ma'am' (as the Princess of Wales must address her) has come to realise that the stewardship of all such matters, in royal as in daily life, is now passing ever more surely into the hands of the young. If one of her grandsons falls for a none-too-suitable starlet, for instance, Queen Elizabeth may cluck with gentle disapproval; but fond indulgence will soon prevail, and have her offering him the privacy of one of her paparazzi-proof homes.

Come what may, the Queen Mother will long symbolise an era which still holds a strong emotional appeal for many Britons, including those born long after its heyday: an era of patriotism and 'the proper thing', of conservative values and churchgoing morals, of formal but close-knit family life, of canasta and charades and country walks, of genteel delight in

The Queen Mother and Princess Diana – two commoners destined to be Queen – watch the Trooping the Colour. It was the Queen Mother who gave Diana, in the early weeks of her engagement to Prince Charles, a 'crash course' in the art of being royal.

good clean fun. It is very much the lifestyle her daughter has inherited, and which her eldest son will in time pass on as the Royal Family's example to the nation. It is, above all, very British. Whatever other fashions come and go, it is a way of life, a set of values, which the majority of Britons will seek to perpetuate – thus erecting an unconscious memorial to a remarkable lady's strength of character.

A warm welcome for Prince Andrew from his grandmother on his return from the Falkland's conflict.

QUEEN MUM

Many people, royalists or not, remain baffled by the mystic thrall in which the British monarchy holds its subjects. Whether they regard the Royal Family as the sacred fount of the nation's authority or merely as characters in a long-running upper-crust soap opera, they are at a loss to explain its hypnotic powers.

The Queen Mother has them doubly baffled. What is it about this petite, soft-spoken old lady, not herself born royal, which has children eating out of her hand and reduces strong men to tears? Which aspect of the national subconscious has people of all stations and degrees revering her, reduced to nervous wrecks in her presence, even dreaming recurring dreams about her walking their dog or dropping in (inevitably without warning, when the house is a terrible mess) for tea?

The answer lies less in who she is than in what she represents. She has lived through all the great events of this century and enjoyed a ringside seat at most, a central role in many. Fate has pitchforked her from a genteel Scottish childhood to a reverent old age in which she hobnobs with prime ministers and potentates and enjoys an international reputation which, unlike theirs, will outlive any merely passing political popularity. At the same time, she can be as down-to-earth as your next-door neighbour; a chat with her is as natural and straightforward as a natter over the garden wall.

It is no loyalist flummery to say that of all the members of the royal family, the Queen Mother is the one who actually *listens* to what is said to her and will invariably make a thoughtful, personal reply. Not for her the ingrained, pre-tailored small talk of some other royals. Queen Elizabeth will

Top: *The closeness of the Royal Family is evident as they leave the church at Sandringham after morning service, January 1969.* Above: *The Queen Mother, on her sixtieth birthday, holds the infant Prince Andrew, her new grandson, in the garden of Clarence House.*

The Queen Mother relaxes with her grandchildren, Prince Charles and Princess Anne, at Royal Lodge, Windsor, 1954.

let you take her gloved hand gently in yours, and will then hold on to you quite firmly while she fixes you in the eye and makes the most of those few seconds of royal contact. She knows how much it means, how long it will be remembered.

Her virtues, in the end, are the simplest ones, those proverbially placed next to godliness. Put them together with rather more earthly pursuits, such as *The Sporting Life*, corgis and fly-fishing, and you have everyone's favourite auntie or granny. Right down to that sly, conspiratorial streak of mischief.

In private, even with close friends, she prefers a proper degree of formality and will insist on correct forms of address and behaviour in 'the presence'. With members of the public, however, she is not as fussed as other royals sometimes are about matters of protocol or etiquette. She is the only one who can commit the royal heresy of referring naturally to 'my daughter' or 'my grandson', rather than speaking archly of 'the Queen' or 'the Prince of Wales'. She may not always start her engagements promptly but she invariably ends them well behind schedule – a sure sign that she has been enjoying herself as much as those she has been meeting. She is never, but never, anything other than entirely natural.

It is a remarkable fact that there is no recorded instance, in her long and active lifetime, of the Queen Mother *ever* having lost her temper – extraordinary in one whose life has been so crowded with detail, not all of it entirely welcome. Those who work for her speak of a very occasional narrowing of the eyes – a fearful chill washing over that sparkling violet-blue – but never of a spoken rebuke, an angry *hauteur*, not even a raised voice.

One of the few names on her unwritten 'blacklist' – of people who have behaved unforgivably – is that of the former president of the United States, Jimmy Carter, 'the only man since my dear husband died to have kissed me on the lips'. Any such slur on the memory of King George VI, either as husband or as monarch, will earn perpetual banishment from the Queen Mother's court. She was outraged when one or two of our more forward newspapers suggested some years ago that she might

The Queen Mother decides to play safe behind the blue – those reds can be tricky – while playing snooker at London's Mayflower Family Centre Youth Club, which she opened in March 1980.

It was only after the King's death that the Queen Mother really developed her enthusiasm for horse-racing. With Devon Loch in the unsaddling enclosure at Sandown Park, December 1955. On the left is trainer Peter Cazalet, on the right jockey Dick Francis, later to become one of the Queen Mother's favourite authors. In the following year Devon Loch was to lose the Grand National in famous and extraordinary circumstances.

remarry. Bachelor members of her own Household – Sir Arthur Penn, then Her Majesty's Comptroller, and Sir Ralph Anstruther, still her Treasurer – were even put forward as potential candidates. Queen Elizabeth, to put it mildly, was not amused.

Above: *The Queen Mother, who has a well-known enthusiasm for flowers, at the Royal National Rose Show, Alexandra Palace, in 1966.* Left: *A keen angler since her girlhood, the Queen Mother is pictured in the Waikato River in Auckland while on a 1966 tour of New Zealand.*

Right: *Two attentive racegoers at the 201st Derby, June 1980 – unlike her mother, the Queen prefers flat racing to steeplechasing.* Below: *A delighted Queen Mother with Sunnyboy after its win at Ascot on 10 April 1975 had brought her winning total to 300 races.*

The pleasures which have consoled her long widowhood have led her into some brave new worlds. Few people realise, for instance, that it was only after her husband's death that she grew really interested in horse-racing: strictly over-the-sticks, unlike her daughter the Queen who prefers the less hectic elegance of the flat-racing season.

The entire nation was rooting for the Queen Mother in 1956, when her horse Devon Loch entered the final straight of the Grand National with a handsome lead, only to 'pancake' yards from the finishing line. Harold Nicolson was there again. 'She never turned a hair,' he recorded. Amid a horrified silence at Aintree she said simply: 'I must go down and comfort those poor people.' To Devon Loch's jockey, Dick Francis, now one of her favourite authors, she said: 'Please don't be upset. That's racing.' Later she sent Francis a silver cigarette box to commemorate the win-that-almost-was, with an inscription so touching that to this day he covers it with his hand as he offers you a cigarette.

It was at another Grand National that the Queen Mother's spontaneity saved a potentially awkward moment. She happened to be standing in the paddock, at the foot of the steps to the BBC commentary box, when Richard Dimbleby emerged for a breather. A royal favourite because of his many ceremonial broadcasts, the corpulent commentator tripped and fell right on top of the venerable figure of the Queen Mother, with whom he found himself in an unceremonious embrace on the Aintree turf. 'Ah, Richard,' she said, gently extracting herself from his mortified clutches, 'I didn't know you cared.'

Many of Queen Elizabeth's happiest, most natural private hours have been spent at the stables of her trainers – once Peter Cazalet, now Fulke Walwyn – where the former Empress can often be found sitting on the most improvised of seats or astride a fence, inconspicuous beneath her headscarf, talking expertly of the thoroughbreds she calls 'my little darlings'. Stable lads have become quite nonchalant about this most celebrated of owners turning up without prior warning in the company of another expert adviser – her daughter, the Queen. The younger

Elizabeth also finds many of her most relaxed, satisfying moments roughing it in the pungent surroundings of racing stables, talking on equal terms with the leading specialists in the field.

The Queen, say those who know both, is probably her mother's most devoted admirer. Elizabeth II talks openly and with genuinely wide eyes of the Queen Mother's wisdom, calmness and, above all, stamina. When the Queen recently told a Commonwealth Prime Minister, in front of an eavesdropping television camera, that she envied her mother's energy and found it hard to keep up with her, she was not just making polite, non-political small talk. Privately, she tells friends that she very much doubts she will herself still be 'going as strong' in her eighties.

It was typical, for instance, that only eight days after an operation under general anaesthetic for the removal of that stubborn fishbone, at the age of eighty-three, the Queen Mother was back on public duty, attending the inaugural meeting of the Court of Patrons of the Royal College of Obstetricians and Gynaecologists. It was only on the insistence of her doctors that she had sadly agreed, earlier that week, to miss out on two of her favourite 'hardy annuals': the Diplomatic Corps reception at Buckingham Palace and the Royal Ballet gala at Covent Garden. Her staff say she has made it 'official policy', all her life, never to admit to feeling cold, tired or ill.

With the inevitability of each passing year the Queen Mother reluctantly sheds one or two of her more arduous appointments, but the annually published figures show her still to be one of the most active members of the Royal Family. Her average of 120-plus public engagements a year exceeds those of all the 'lesser' (not to say younger) royals – everyone, that is, except the Queen herself, Prince Philip, Prince Charles and Princess Anne.

Whenever she accepts an engagement – you never know your luck, but anything to do with young people, music or medicine is likely to catch her eye – her staff will always telephone the local Lord Lieutenant to see if there is anything else useful she can do while she is in the area. A visit? An opening? An unveiling? The Queen Mother has always liked to make the most of an excursion by converting one engagement into three or four. An advance party from Clarence House will vet HM's proposed route in advance, check out the guest list and offer helpful little bits of advice to hosts. Yes, Her Majesty will accept a 'g-&-t' – in private, of course – but drinks wine only with meals. No, she won't eat much. Sir Dingle Foot, brother of the former Labour leader Michael, was once surprised to find himself confronted by a *brace* of partridge at a formal London dinner; further enquiries of his neighbour, the Queen Mother, revealed that the guest of honour had deftly slid the unwanted bird from her plate to his.

If venturing outside London (which, even these days, is more often than not) she still loves to travel by helicopter – always her favourite form of transport. She will think nothing of a two- or three-hour 'walkabout' before putting her feet up in the Rolls or Daimler (one of each, both growing rather old) which will take her on to her next appointment. Even then she will usually wind down the window to give everyone a final, farewell glimpse not just of her smile but of that famous royal wave – the definitive version, never quite emulated by other leading royals, despite its inventor's helpful advice that 'it should look like you're unscrewing one of those large jars of sweets'.

Of her innumerable public offices and titles, the one which has given the Queen Mother most pleasure in recent years was the Chancellorship of the University of London, to which she devoted great time and trouble before retiring at the age of eighty (when she was delighted to be succeeded by her granddaughter, Princess Anne). It was the beginning, say those around her, of the unofficial 'crusade for youth' which has preoccupied her old age. With each year that she herself grows older, she concentrates more and more on her work for the young.

The same is true, even less officially, within her family. Each new engagement, wedding or birth affords her particular pleasure, above all those recent ones in direct line to the throne. Having guided the Princess of Wales through her first,

The Queen Mother celebrated her eightieth birthday, 4 August 1980, by appearing outside Clarence House with other members of the Royal Family and waving to cheering crowds. Behind the Queen Mother are Princess Margaret's son, Viscount Linley, Prince Edward and Prince Charles.

tentative public steps, the Queen Mother has since been the first to applaud hereffortless mastery of the tricky art of becoming royal. One distant day, it is not unreasonable to suppose, that same young lady may well find herself a Queen Dowager, a King Mother, and look back for inspiration to the example of Elizabeth Bowes-Lyon, daughter of the 14th Earl of Strathmore, who became – despite herself – Duchess of York, Queen Consort to King George VI, Queen Mother to Queen Elizabeth II, and one of the most popular 'royals' of all time. It will be a tough act to follow.

Queen Elizabeth has never sought any reward for her devotion to duty, and so was doubly moved on her eightieth

The Christening of Prince Henry, the Queen Mother's great-grandson. Prince Henry was born on 15 September 1984 and was christened on 21 December in St George's Chapel, Windsor.

birthday when no fewer than 30,000 cards, telegrams or messages of congratulations came in from all over the world. Her eighty-fifth birthday will no doubt see that record broken.

As old as the century and as spry as ever, she may yet be spared to fulfil the promise she has teasingly made to her staff. The Queen Mother is determined to reach her 100th birthday – so she can receive a telegram from the Queen.